JOHNNY

CA

JOHNNY CASH

The Life and Legacy of the Man in Black

ALAN LIGHT

SMITHSONIAN BOOKS

WASHINGTON, DC

CON1

FOREWORD

Johnny Cash may be the best example of a performer who had no line between the music and the man. The songs he sang sounded like him and embodied him in every way. There are artists who are nothing like their personas, but Cash really was the characters he sang about. He wasn't a felon, but he did get locked up now and then. Although he didn't write "Ring of Fire," it is entirely him—a victim of temptation. His music was born of who he was as a man.

He didn't just contribute to country music—he built it. He was what I would consider a founding father. Hank Williams arguably invented what we think of as modern country music, but then Johnny took that same clay and made it into something unique and even more interesting.

I think in some ways Hank gave his life for an entire format—he completely immersed himself in heartbreak so we could all enjoy the songs that were born of his tragic story. But if Hank was the messiah come to bring us the music and die for it, Cash was like the apostle Paul: the one who would expand it, relate it, spread the word around the world. He took it further than anyone thought possible at the time. The person most responsible for the worldwide perception of what country music is—and what's great about it—is probably Johnny Cash.

The most inspiring thing about him, to me, is that he got his life right—or, as he would probably say, June got his life right, and turned him into the man he was capable of being. And what a turnaround it was. The authorities and his friends had all but given up hope for him. Here was a man who struggled mightily, who overcame these setbacks—from a vocal teacher who basically told him to hang it up, to addiction and intense heartbreak—but who was also the first to see that these weren't necessarily obstacles God had put before him. He recognized that he'd built his own obstacles, and so he overcame them.

I was fortunate enough to work on an unfinished Johnny Cash song for the *Forever Words* album. For the video, John Carter Cash, Johnny and June's son, gave me some home movies to include. They showed the family at the Grand Canyon, Johnny taking pictures like any other husband and father on vacation. It was a side of him I'd never seen, and I was taken aback by the intense reality of it, by the love he had for his family. I think people will get a lot of that feeling from the photographs in this book.

But as real and normal as his life appeared, he still had *it*, whatever *it* is. He was on vacation, his kids running around like some normal suburban family from Duluth or Paducah, but he was still Johnny Cash. No one ever looked cooler on vacation. Very few people have that much charisma. It's fascinating to look at this candid stuff and wonder, was he ever not the Johnny Cash we worship and revere?

One fascinating thing I've noticed is how new generations constantly rediscover this man's music. I think little kids instinctively like Johnny Cash. I know I did. They like that deep voice, that lower-frequency gut punch. They can sense he was ornery, a kindred youthful spirit; they can hear that smile, that wink in his music. We put him on a pedestal as a serious legend, as if he's almost made out of granite, but I know he was a real character who loved life and laughter.

I just shot a little video in California for a benefit show for first responders. I was at a small fire station with my acoustic guitar, and I asked what they wanted me to play. The firefighters were calling out for some of my songs, but a little four-year-old girl named Maren spoke up and asked, "Can you play any Johnny Cash?"

And a little child shall lead them. There's hope for the world right there, knowing the music and the legend live on. And there is so much more to be discovered about who Cash really was in the pages of this book.

BRAD PAISLEY

I'VE BEEN EVERY WHERE

1

"I worked on this album in spite of everything," Johnny Cash said to me. "I found strength to work just to spite this disease. I came to the studio and I couldn't sing—there were times I came in with no voice, when I could have stayed at home and pouted in my room and cried in my beer or my milk, but

I didn't let that happen. "I came in and opened up my mouth and tried to let something come out. I recorded when it was the last thing in the world I thought I could do. And those are the songs that have the feeling and the fire and the fervor and the passion—there's a great deal of strength coming out of that weakness. 99

CHAPTER OPENER
Cash plays guitar on
the TV series *Ranch
Party*, ca. 1966

It was August of 2002, and I was sitting across a simple kitchen table from one of America's most beloved icons—the Man in Black, the voice of "I Walk the Line" and "Ring of Fire" and "Folsom Prison Blues"—in the "Cash Cabin," a retreat/recording studio he had built in the late 1970s, deep in the woods in Hendersonville, Tennessee, across the road from his primary residence overlooking Old Hickory Lake. The small wooden box was the space where, for the past decade, he had come to write and rehearse songs and record demos for the series of bold, defiant albums that resulted in one of music's unlikeliest final acts.

This day, I was there to record an interview with Cash that would be sent out to radio stations across the country, since he was in no shape to make the usual promotional rounds in person. The assignment was to talk about the soon-to-be-released *American IV: The Man Comes Around* record— the latest installment in the "American Recordings" series spearheaded by young, renegade producer Rick Rubin, and the final music that would be issued during Cash's lifetime. The album included the version of Nine Inch Nails' song "Hurt" that would serve (along with its harrowing, unforgettable music video) as his stunning epitaph.

The singer had recently turned seventy years old and had been struggling with his health for more than a decade. His condition and its severity had repeatedly been misdiagnosed—first as Parkinson's disease, then as MSA (Multiple System Atrophy, formerly called Shy-Drager Syndrome). "Now they say it's something called autonomic neuropathy," says Cash. "I'm not sure what that means, except I think it means that you're getting old and shaky, your immune system gets weaker, the smaller nerves in your extremities stop working." He moved haltingly and needed to take a break from our conversation and rest every fifteen or twenty minutes, but his mind was clear and his focus was sharp.

"We brought a pocketful of songs to every session," he said, "and if I couldn't sing this one, I'd sing that one. In the middle of taping something that wasn't quite working, I'd just stop what I was doing and start a new song. And that always worked—to alternate, to go to something that I could do. The Sting song ["I Hung My Head"], I came to that with practically no voice at all, and I said to myself, 'I will do this song, I know I can do it.'

"It talks about a brother and a brother dying and a rifle and shooting— and I'm kinda into that," he continued. "Well, I was before. I guess I'm a little shaky now, better not shoot at a tree or I might hit a cow. But it's that kind of song that I like, that mournful, tragic song. The songs of my people, a lot of them are songs of disaster and tragedy, murder, death, dying, and broken love affairs, and this song of Sting's just fit right in there."

Death and dying were close to the surface for Cash at this moment, even though he had no way of knowing that just over a year later, he would be gone from this earth—or, more shockingly, that his wife June Carter Cash, his greatest source of strength and support, whom he had long credited for

The Cash family cabin on Cash Estate grounds, Hendersonville, Tennessee. Cash made many of his later recordings at the studio here.

saving his life, would pass away first, in the spring of 2003. (Their relationship would serve as the framework for the acclaimed 2005 film *Walk the Line*, which became the highest-grossing music biopic of all time and won Reese Witherspoon an Oscar for her portrayal of June.) Of course, death had always been a part of Cash's writing; his work was grounded in the harsh realities of existence, the fundamental lessons he had learned growing up on a hardscrabble family farm. Toil (both physical and emotional) and loss were always present in his work, from "Five Feet High and Rising" to "A Boy Named Sue."

But when young men write about death, it is usually somehow romantic. And among pop songwriters, mortality has usually been approached with a combination of fascination, fear, and fantasy, from Jan and Dean's 1964 hit "Dead Man's Curve" to the entire Goth movement.

Johnny Cash, though, never sounded adolescent when he sang about dying. He was twenty-five when he wrote one of his finest songs, "Big River," and when he delivered these lines—"The tears that I cried for that woman

Cash in the Cash Cabin studio, Hendersonville, Tennessee, January 2001

are gonna flood you, big river/Then I'm gonna sit right here until I die"—it didn't seem hyperbolic or stylized; it felt clear-eyed and resolute.

So hearing Cash talk matter-of-factly about aging and death was no surprise. More remarkable at this late stage of his career was his tone when he spoke about his art, his creative renaissance, and the recent expansion of his audience. Almost fifty years after making his first record, he sounded competitive, engaged, proud of his work—he sounded fired up. "We're very protective of it, we watch our flanks," he told me. "We record our stuff, we have whoever we want to on the record, and we take no prisoners. We do it the way we want to."

"JOHNNY WAS AND IS THE NORTH STAR," wrote his friend Bob Dylan after Cash died. "You could guide your ship by him—the greatest of the greats, then and now.... Listen to him, and he always brings you to your senses."

The scope of Johnny Cash's achievement is almost inconceivable. Born in rural poverty in 1932, he would go on to sell almost a hundred million records worldwide. He is recognized first and foremost, of course, as one of the definitive figures in country music. He redefined and revitalized the genre, broadening its possibilities while remaining firmly rooted in the real-life concepts that spoke to and for its listeners. Cash scholar Michael Streissguth wrote that while Hank Williams became the quintessential figure in country music, "there would be no other until Johnny Cash reached his own apogee.... Cash at his peak had given a thunderous jolt to the themes that, in the early twentieth century, first launched and popularized country music."

Cash's music, though, crossed multiple genres—rock and roll, blues, folk, gospel—giving him the rare distinction of being inducted into the Country Music, Rock and Roll, and Gospel Music Halls of Fame. He is, in fact, the only country artist inducted into the Rock Hall as a "performer"—the other country members went in as "early influences."

Keith Richards of the Rolling Stones is usually described as the world's leading acolyte of rock and roll pioneer Chuck Berry. But he once told journalist Anthony DeCurtis that "if someone came up to me and for some reason they could only get a collection of one person's music, I'd say 'Chuck Berry is important, but man, you've got to get the Cash.'"

In country song after country song since Cash's death, there's a steady lament that the form has lost the sense of honor and creativity that the Man in Black represented. His name and story are constantly invoked in lyrics (George Strait's "House of Cash," Jason Aldean's "Johnny Cash," Shelby Lynne's "Johnny Met June"). In "Long Time Gone" the Dixie Chicks described how Nashville performers are lacking—"They got money, but they don't have Cash."

And then there was that voice, unlike anything we have heard before or since. A low, rumbling baritone, it sounded both deeply intimate and like a proclamation from the heavens. It's hard to imagine that, when he was growing up, anyone would have expected that his singing would make him a star—that sound, undoubtedly arresting, was far from conventional. But his stentorian, penetrating tone was a landmark in the transition to popular singers with more idiosyncratic deliveries. What mattered wasn't his vocal range but his sincerity; no matter what he was singing, first and foremost Cash always sounded honest.

As an author, actor, and moral compass as well, his impact went beyond his sound, and was recognized with some of the highest honors in the land. In 1996, Cash received the Kennedy Center Honors, and three years later, he was given the GRAMMY Lifetime Achievement Award. In 2001, he was awarded the National Medal of Arts, the nation's highest honor specifically given for achievement in the arts on behalf of the people.

Ultimately, Johnny Cash meant more than his songs. He was an almost impossible amalgam of everything that America had to offer, for better and for worse. He was a man of faith who stood up to authority; a drug addict

American rebels: Cash making trouble with
Muhammad Ali and Waylon Jennings, late 1970s

embraced by both parents and children; a defender of the downtrodden who was welcomed at penitentiaries and in the White House.

"He was almost biblical," said Sheryl Crow, "because he walked this earth and experienced all a man could suffer." Tom Petty, a longtime friend and sometime collaborator, explained Cash's fundamental appeal, the credibility of his message, another way. "He was the man that we would all like to be," the late singer-songwriter once said. "If you've got to bust it down to one word, it's integrity."

Even such an unlikely disciple as 2017's breakout rapper-singer Post Malone keeps the flame burning for Cash. He sports a large tattoo of Cash on one bicep and told Vice that "Johnny Cash influenced me a lot. He's a great

Johnny and June Cash with actor and football
player Rosey Grier in Los Angeles, late 1970s

storyteller. I've always loved the live San Quentin performance—just the
pure joy that you can see from all the people that were in jail, that Johnny
came to rock with them and show 'em some love, is really inspiring." In
2018, Lenny Kravitz announced that his next album would include a "psychedelic funk meets country" song titled "Johnny Cash," recalling his own
encounter with the singer.

He was beloved by hippies and homemakers, punks and preachers,
somehow creating a mosaic of fans that transcended the socially polarized
1960s (and seems all the more incredible in the twenty-first-century United
States). At the pinnacle of his popularity, Cash attained something like a
true universality. In 1969—a year in which he placed no fewer than nine

albums on the pop charts and began hosting a groundbreaking network television show—he and Muhammad Ali were the best-known people in the world, according to *Life* magazine. The Beatles and the Pope were as recognizable, the publication noted, but not by name.

His friend and associate Kris Kristofferson wrote a line in his 1971 song "The Pilgrim, Chapter 33" that is widely assumed to be at least partially based on Cash—"He's a walking contradiction, partly truth and partly fiction/ Taking every wrong direction on his lonely way back home." But maybe even more applicable are Walt Whitman's famous words from "Song of Myself"— "Do I contradict myself?/ Very well then I contradict myself,/ (I am large, I contain multitudes)." It is no wonder, then, that Cash once stated, "Nothing ever written about me has told it right."

Along the way, he came to stand for something like America itself. Robert Frank, the singular photographer and filmmaker whose 1959 series *The Americans* created a transformative vision of the country and its citizens, described moving to the United States from his native Switzerland. "It takes a long time to come from another culture, from Europe, and come here and get used to America," he said. "The first record I bought was Johnny Cash."

Almost fifteen years after his death, Cash's status as a man who spoke to people of all stripes, and whose words and image still held power and meaning across the political and social spectrum, was back in the headlines. In August of 2017, a video was posted of a self-proclaimed neo-Nazi delivering a message of racial hatred in the midst of the "Unite the Right" rally in Charlottesville, Virginia. In the clip, the young man was wearing a Johnny Cash T-shirt. Cash's children posted their response a few days later on Facebook.

"Johnny Cash was a man whose heart beat with the rhythm of love and social justice," read the statement, which was signed by Rosanne, Kathy, Cindy, Tara, and John Carter Cash. "He received humanitarian awards from, among others, the Jewish National Fund, B'nai Brith, and the United Nations. He championed the rights of Native Americans, protested the war in Vietnam, was a voice for the poor, the struggling and the disenfranchised, and an advocate for the rights of prisoners. . . . He would be horrified at even a casual use of his name or image for an idea or a cause founded in persecution and hatred.

"Our dad told each of us, over and over throughout our lives, 'Children, you can choose love or hate. I choose love.'

"To any who claim supremacy over other human beings, to any who believe in racial or religious hierarchy: we are not you. Our father, as a person, icon, or symbol, is not you. We ask that the Cash name be kept far away from destructive and hateful ideology."

And yet the sense that Johnny Cash—with his classic agrarian upbringing, working-class country music fan base, and unwavering independence— could also represent repellent and racist attitudes somehow persevered. Is it, in some ways, a tribute to the voice he offers to those who feel voiceless,

Filming ABC's *Johnny Cash Show* with June Carter Cash on location at Cummins Prison Farm, Arkansas, April 10, 1969

even those who miss his fundamental message? The following month, Cash's record labels sent a cease-and-desist letter to *Stormfront Radio*, the weekly radio show for the white supremacist site Stormfront, regarding its use of his version of Tom Petty's "I Won't Back Down."

Cash's son John Carter spoke to *Rolling Stone* about the situation, saying that he was "unsettled and upset" after learning through a fan about the show's usage of the song.

"We do not let slip from our understanding that America was founded on a bonding of many people, from many places and of various color and religions," he said. "We learned this philosophy directly from our father."

John Carter went on: "So many use Dad's name, saying 'Johnny Cash would not like this' or 'Johnny Cash would do this' or 'Johnny Cash would vote for….' Please, let his actions speak for who he was: a simple, loving man who never supported hate or bigotry. He was nonpolitical, and a patriot with no public political party affiliation."

He sang of the glory of Jesus, and he sang that he shot a man in Reno just to watch him die. He sang of lust and of devotion. He sang of family values and of social injustice. He studied history and honored tradition, but he never stopped evolving. Over the course of five decades as a recording artist, Johnny Cash—true to his roots on the farm—staked out territory that stands as a challenge to other artists of all kinds.

"To be that extraordinary and that ordinary was his real gift," said Bono. "Every man could relate to him, but nobody could be him."

"COUNTRY LIFE AS I KNEW IT might really be a thing of the past," Johnny Cash wrote in his second memoir, *Cash: The Autobiography* (coauthored with journalist Patrick Carr), "and when music people today, performers and fans alike, talk about being 'country,' they don't mean they know or even care about the land and the life it sustains and regulates."

No doubt that he was right about the influx of suburban cowboys and hard-partying frat boys who would continue to dominate the country charts. And in 2017, to pay a visit to Cash's hometown of Dyess, Arkansas, is indeed to travel back to a different time in American history. To a casual (urban) eye, it doesn't seem like much has changed since the Cash family moved there when their fourth and middle child was just a toddler, in 1935. Maybe there's a smoother way into town—maybe it was just the setting on my GPS—but my final approach to Dyess from the Memphis airport, about an hour away, took me through several miles of unpaved roads, through the middle of endless cotton fields, with chickens scrambling to get out of the road in front of me and a big cloud of dust in my wake. Although there is one change—to get to the house Cash grew up in, you take a road that's been renamed Johnny Cash Highway—still, you make the final turn when you get to a cotton gin.

I've come to Arkansas for the three-day inaugural Johnny Cash Heritage Festival, the latest event in an ongoing celebration and exploration of

House 266, Road 3: Cash's childhood home in
the experimental community of Dyess, Arkansas

the singer's early life and the historic community in which he was raised.
The Dyess Colony, established in 1934, was one of the nation's earliest and
largest agricultural resettlement communities under the New Deal. In 2011,
Arkansas State University (ASU), with the support and involvement of the
Cash family, began staging a series of concerts to raise funds for the acquisition and restoration of Cash's boyhood home. In 2014, the refurbished
residence was opened to the public, and since then, other buildings have
been fixed up and historic markers added around town. Funds from this
year's event target the re-creation of the barn, smokehouse, chicken coop,
and privy that once were a part of the Cash farmstead.

The 2017 festival—which draws 3,000 Cash devotees, including visitors
from Scotland, the Netherlands, Ireland, and Austria—consists of several
days of panels and presentations about the colony's history and its favorite

Outtake from the photo shoot for *Now, There Was a Song!*, one of Cash's first albums on Columbia Records, San Antonio, Texas, 1959

son. Dr. Micki Pulleyking, a religious studies professor at Missouri State University, discusses "Cash's contributions to theopoetics through his songwriting." Three members of the Dyess High School Class of 1950 offer their recollections of Cash, the class vice president.In the evenings, local musicians perform on a makeshift stage at the town's center, the Dyess Colony Circle.

During a break from the lectures, as families shuffle around the circle eating hamburgers or checking out some local produce, the crew tests the sound system, and out comes the voice of Cash singing "Hurt," one of the most anguished recordings imaginable. As kids look for sodas and grandparents retreat to the benches for shade, the soundtrack is that unmistakable growl grimly intoning "I focus on the pain/The only thing that's real." The inherent complications of honoring a figure as expansive as Johnny Cash are always close to the surface.

On Saturday morning, his first-born child, the GRAMMY-winning singer-songwriter Rosanne Cash, introduces the speaker for the "Featured Presentations" and offers a few thoughts to the attendees about returning to her father's home. "His southern poetry and sense of rhythm came from that black earth he worked," she says, and recounts his feeling that "every rock, tree, stump is precious to me." She adds, "This is just remarkable. Talk about time travel...."

Later that afternoon, Rosanne headlines the festival's main event, a concert that takes place in the Sunken Fields immediately adjacent to the residence. The house is small and tidy (one of the panelists notes that it's been restored and presented at its "Sunday best")—it's about 1,000 square feet, with a kitchen, living room, dining room, bathroom, and two bedrooms. There was no electricity and no running water. The sleeping quarters look pleasant and comfortable enough, although this modest house slept nine people—Ray and Carrie Cash and their seven children. (After the festival the house was added to the National Register of Historic Places.) The most important thing to remember is that it was where Johnny Cash formed his view of the world, a distinctive and uncompromising perspective that would go on to touch and influence millions of people.

Standing on the back porch and looking across the fields, what remains palpable is the feeling of isolation. There's nothing but flat earth and land as far as you can see, and it's easy to imagine both the long stretches of time to be filled up with words and music by a dreamy, poetic boy and his desperate need to escape.

Rosanne notes that it was a "dream to bring music back to the fields"— the very site her grandfather planted with cotton. Under sunny skies (with minimal shade), an audience of 2,500 gathers for performances starting with one-time *Nashville Star* winner Buddy Jewell, who was born in neighboring Lepanto, and Cash's younger siblings Joanne and Tommy, both recording artists as well. The stage is set up no more than fifty yards from the house— both structures fit easily in the frame of a camera.

The day's most remarkable set comes from Kris Kristofferson. At age eighty-one, the legendary songwriter has been battling illness for several years; for a while, his memory loss was assumed to be Alzheimer's disease, but a subsequent diagnosis revealed that it was the effect of Lyme disease. Since then, medication has stabilized his decline and he's been able to perform regularly, though his short-term memory remains compromised.

Physically, though, Kristofferson looks fantastic, and he seems strong and in command onstage as long as he sticks to the set list carefully written out for him. He bangs through twenty-one songs over the course of an hour, including such masterpieces from his catalogue as "Me and Bobby McGee," "Help Me Make It Through the Night" (named by David Cantwell and Bill Friskics-Warren as the greatest country song of all time in their invaluable book, *Heartaches by the Number*), and "For the Good Times."

Most powerful in this setting are the songs Kristofferson wrote that are associated with Cash. He sings "The Pilgrim" (with its "walking contradiction" line) and several of his compositions that Cash had hits with, including "Why Me, Lord" and the masterful "Sunday Morning Coming Down." Given his condition, it's unclear whether Kristofferson knows the significance of these moments or if he's just running down the songs by muscle memory. Other than greeting the crowd with "Hello, Sunken Fields!," he makes no acknowledgment of the circumstances and doesn't speak other than to invite Rosanne onstage for a duet on "Loving Her Was Easier (Than Anything I'll Ever Do Again)." That number was a live staple of the supergroup the Highwaymen, which consisted of Cash, Kristofferson, Willie Nelson, and Waylon Jennings.

Finally, as the sun starts to sink in the sky, Rosanne Cash and her band take the stage. Rosanne, sometime author and professor in addition to her long career as a Gold-selling country star, has been eloquent throughout the weekend in speaking about what this event and this location mean to her, but she's inevitably also been distracted by logistics and details. Now she has nothing to hide behind, as she looks directly at the spot where her father was raised.

"In 2011, when I got involved with ASU," she says, "I was so moved by what I saw and felt down here. To see the house your parent grew up in, the bed they slept in—when your parent is gone, it changes you. It's profound, it's a deep connection, and I feel a deep connection to this place."

Backed by her touring group, led by her husband and frequent collaborator John Leventhal, she delivers a set that often evokes her father's memory—as her shows unavoidably do night after night. She sings Hank Snow's "I'm Movin' On," which she recorded for her 2009 album, *The List*, consisting of material she chose out of a list of 100 essential country songs that her father had given to her when she was eighteen. She plays a killer version of Johnny's 1961 hit "Tennessee Flat-Top Box," with a lengthy solo by Leventhal. As Rosanne performs "Long Black Veil," one of the most enduring and haunting songs in American music—originally recorded by Lefty Frizzell, it's been covered by such artists as The Band, Mick Jagger, Dave Matthews, Bruce Springsteen, Jerry Garcia, and multiple times by Johnny Cash—on the side of the stage Kris Kristofferson happily nuzzles a tiny dog belonging to Joanne Cash and murmurs along with the chorus.

How to imagine what's going through Rosanne Cash's mind? The connections being made explicit, concrete, between her family, her heritage, her music? To close the show, all the performers, plus Rosanne's daughter Carrie (three generations of Cashes onstage now), gather to sing "Will the Circle Be Unbroken," the hymn closely associated with the Carter Family—which, of course, brings the spirit and history of June Carter Cash to the concert as well.

When Johnny Cash and I talked in Hendersonville in 2002 about his new album, *American IV: The Man Comes Around*, he said that it "goes in so

"To me, it was luxuries untold": Cash in the
backyard of his boyhood house in Dyess; outtake
from *Look* magazine photo shoot, 1968

many different directions, but they all come together, and where they come
together is in a one-ness with me. They come together in being my songs."

The fields in Dyess, the dirt, the sky, the silence all shaped his writing
and his music, but beyond that, they grounded Cash in basic human truths
that he was able to translate into art and action, creating a sense of "one-
ness with me" that resonated across class and culture, and leaving a legacy
that reshaped America.

"Truly, he is what the land and country are all about," wrote Bob Dylan,
"the heart and soul of it personified and what it means to be here."

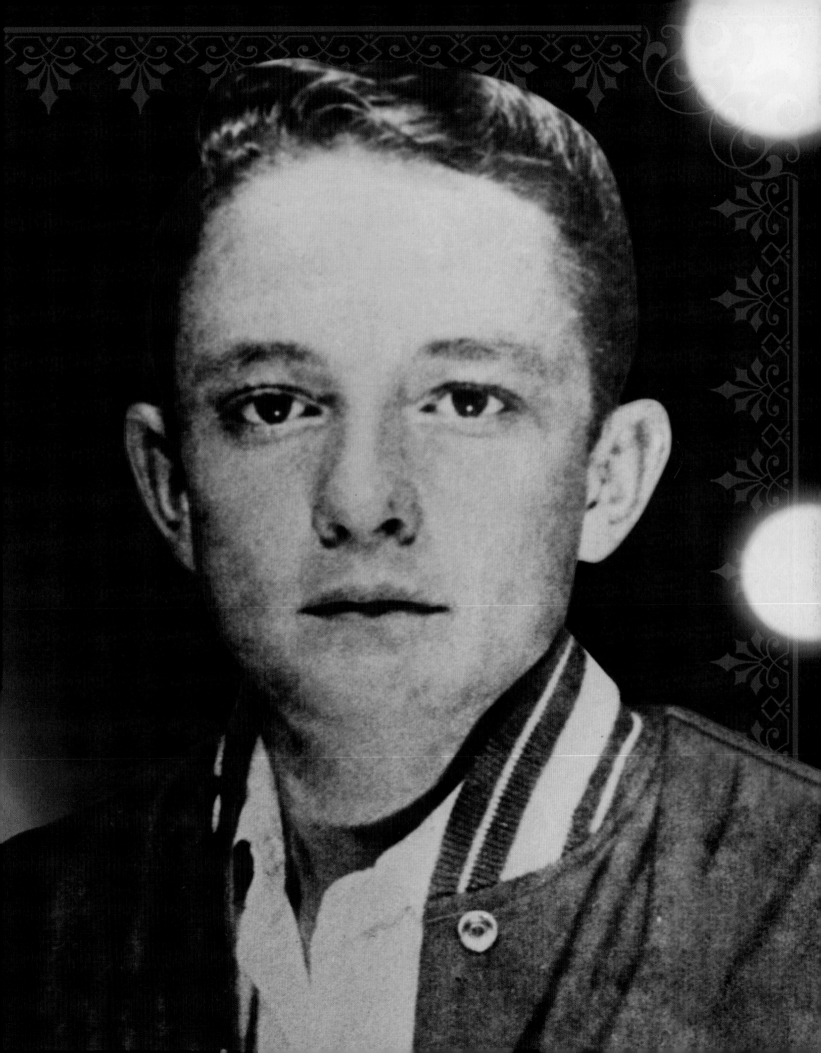

1932–1954

"My work life has been simple," Johnny Cash wrote; "cotton as a youth and music as an adult."

In his autobiography, Cash traced his lineage back to the first king of Scotland. But his own upbringing was a far cry from that of any kind of royalty or landed gentry. He was born on February 26, 1932, in Kingsland, Arkansas—a new spot on the map, built around a railroad stop—to Ray and Carrie Cash. He was the fourth of seven children: Roy, Louise, and Jack preceded him, and Reba, Joanne, and Tommy would follow.

At birth, his mother wanted to name him John (after her father), and his dad was pushing for Ray Junior. Because they were unable to reach a decision, he was listed as "J. R. Cash" on his birth certificate (it would be pronounced by Arkansas locals as one syllable, closer to "Jar"). Not until he enlisted in the military, when he was required to fill out a full name, did he become "John" in any formalized way. Michael Streissguth's research, however, turned up the fact that in the 1940 census, the Cash household lists a boy named John—so perhaps Carrie had prevailed in the end.

Ray Cash was a struggling farmer and itinerant laborer. He had served in France during World War I but didn't see action; in fact, the most notable moment in his service came when he lost a train that he was supposed to be guarding. In the 1974 television special *Ridin' the Rails: The Great American Train Story*, which Johnny hosted, he reminisced about the days of hobos jumping trains, "men moving on to look for any kind of work they

Cash with friends, Dyess, Arkansas, 1948

could get." In a strikingly personal moment for a historical documentary, he went on to offer that "my daddy would be one of these working hobos, and the Depression years would be awfully hard on him." In fact, one of Johnny's earliest memories was of his father leaping out of a moving boxcar and rolling down into a ditch, returning home from riding the freights in search of work when there wasn't cotton to pick.

The Cashes lived in a classic shotgun shack in the woods outside of Kingsland. In 1933, the Federal Emergency Relief Administration (FERA) program was launched as part of the New Deal to provide grants to state governments for a variety of projects in fields such as agriculture, the arts, construction, and education—including a plan through which farmers who had been ruined by the Depression could resettle on land that the government had purchased. The first of these forty-six experimental settlement projects was the Dyess Colony in Mississippi County, Arkansas, which was established in 1934 to give 500 families (whites only) a new start. The roads were laid out as concentric circles, with a town center that had such gathering points as a city hall, movie theater, and restaurant. "We heard that we could buy twenty acres of land with no money down," Ray Cash said, "and a house and a barn, and they would give us a mule and a cow and furnish groceries through the first year until we had a crop and could pay it back."

Cash historian Mark Stielper points out that to get a sense of how miserable life was in Cleveland County, where the Cashes were living, consider the fact that when word was sent out about the opportunity to move to a nameless swamp, the whole town lined up to escape. The application process for Dyess was rigorous, and the Cash family was not on the original list of those approved, but they were eventually cleared. In March 1935, they made the two-day trip (the cost of which was put on their tab—though the colony was an attempt at "communalism," it was far from a free ride) to move 250 miles into a new home, a new town, and a new experiment.

House 266 on Road 3 had no electricity and no running water. There were five cans of paint left on the floor for the new tenants to pretty up the place. On Rosanne Cash's GRAMMY-winning 2014 album, *The River and the Thread*, she sings about the house on the song "The Sunken Lands," opening with the line "Five cans of paint in the empty fields"; when she introduced this song onstage at the festival in Dyess, she said that "the hero of this song is my grandmother—she raised seven children, picked cotton in these fields, was married to a man who could be unkind, and she never complained."

Johnny Cash described the new house as "to me, luxuries untold." His classmate A. J. Henson said that for his family, "moving to Dyess was like dying and going to heaven—it was beyond our wildest dreams."

The Cashes' allocated twenty acres were a tangled, soupy, overgrown mess; Ray put on his rain gear, walked the land, and declared it to be good. The family set to work hacking through the trees and vines; by the start of the planting season that first year, they had been able to clear only about three acres. They stripped the grass from the yard around the house because of the snakes. J.R. started working in the fields as a water boy and was dragging a cotton sack by age eight. Eventually, Ray determined that twenty acres wasn't going to be sufficient economically and was able to double the size of his lot.

Cash would romanticize his connection to the land for the rest of his days; in his autobiography, he compared the rural beauty and simplicity of Cinnamon Hill, his house in Jamaica, to his childhood home in Arkansas, and he also kept some kind of farm that he could tend to, however recreationally, throughout his life. But the work in Dyess was brutal, relentless. At least twice during Cash's youth, the Tyronza River flooded and wiped out

LEFT The Rivers family, Johnny's relatives on his mother's (Carrie Cloveree Cash) side, at a reunion, Kingsland, Arkansas, 1955. Johnny's sister Joanne is the dark-haired woman in the front row, next to his brother Roy Cash and his cousin Horace Rivers on the far right. **RIGHT** Ray and Carrie Cash at grave of their son Jack Cash, Bassett Cemetery, Arkansas, 1944. "My father was an enigma to me—the most interesting specter in my memories," Johnny once recalled.

crops. Though he didn't record the song "Five Feet High and Rising" until 1959, its lyrics ("It's already over all the wheat and the oats/Two feet high and rising." … "Cow's in water up past her knees/Three feet high and rising") were directly inspired by the flood of 1937. "'Five Feet High and Rising' came from my own experience, not some story book," he wrote.

The most complicated relationship in young J.R.'s life, which in many ways never fully left him, was—like that of so many men—with his father. In his first memoir, 1975's *Man in Black*, Cash had only positive things to say about Ray, who was still alive at the time and a grandfather to young John Carter Cash, Johnny's only son. But when he wrote his second autobiography, *Cash: The Autobiography*, in 1997, his father had been dead for more than a decade, and Johnny painted a decidedly different picture.

"I [have] memories of times when his ways could be harsh," Cash wrote. "He never once told me he loved me, and he never had a loving hand to lay

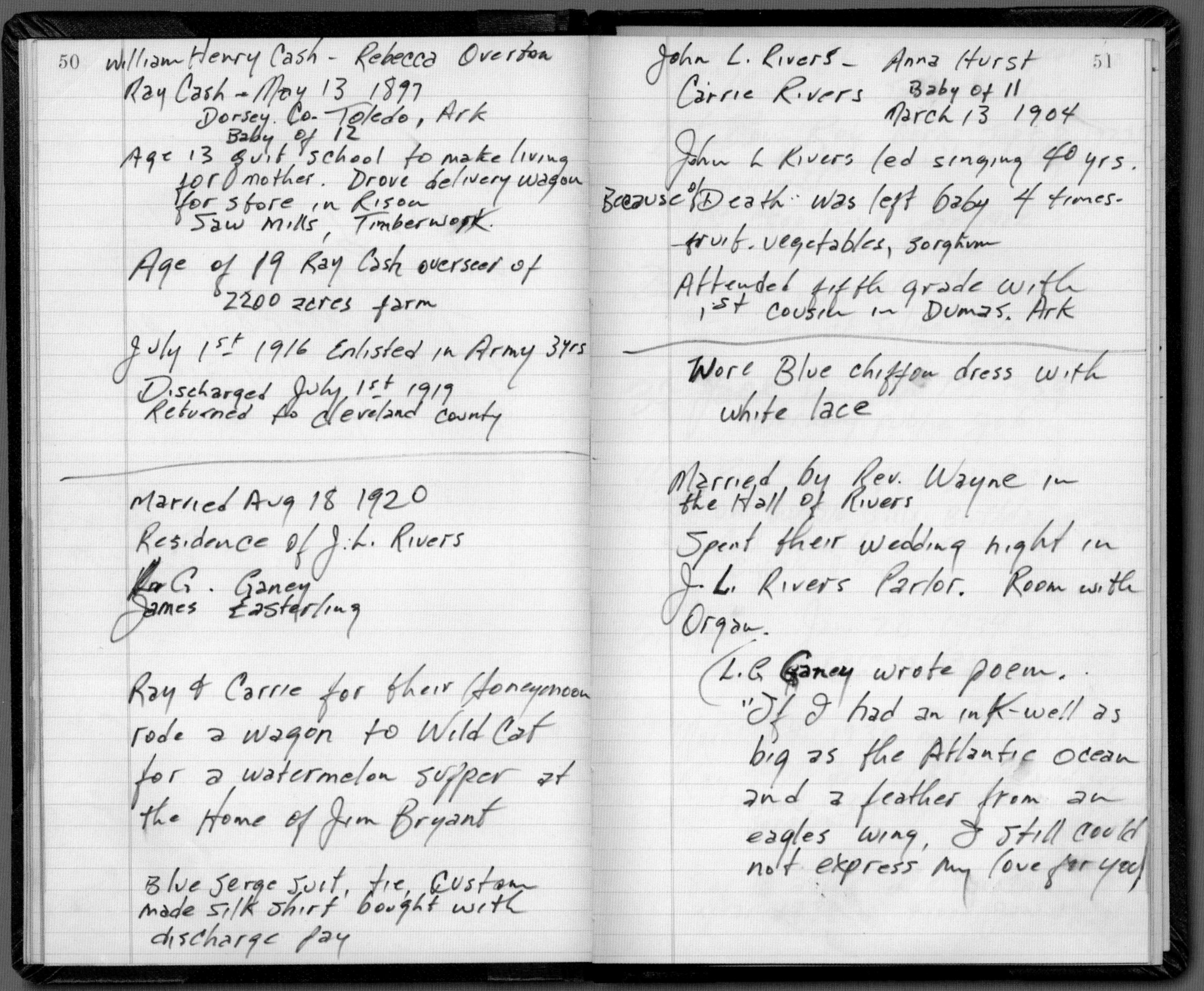

William Henry Cash - Rebecca Overton
Ray Cash - May 13 1897
Dorsey Co. Toledo, Ark
Baby of 12
Age 13 quit school to make living
for mother. Drove delivery wagon
for store in Rison
Saw Mills, Timberwork.

Age of 19 Ray Cash overseer of
2200 acres farm

July 1st 1916 Enlisted in Army 3 yrs
Discharged July 1st 1919
Returned to Cleveland county

Married Aug 18 1920
Residence of J.L. Rivers
Rev. G. Ganey
James Easterling

Ray & Carrie for their Honeymoon
rode a wagon to Wild Cat
for a watermelon supper at
the Home of Jim Bryant

Blue serge suit, tie, Custom
made silk shirt bought with
discharge pay

John L. Rivers - Anna Hurst
Carrie Rivers Baby of 11
March 13 1904
John L Rivers led singing 40 yrs.
Because of Death was left baby 4 times-
fruit. vegetables, sorghum

Attended fifth grade with
1st cousin in Dumas. Ark

Wore Blue chiffon dress with
white lace

Married by Rev. Wayne in
the Hall of Rivers
Spent their wedding night in
J. L. Rivers Parlor. Room with
Organ.

L.C. Ganey wrote poem.
"If I had an ink-well as
big as the Atlantic ocean
and a feather from an
eagles wing, I still could
not express my love for you"

Cash's handwritten notes on his family history. "He
was a scholar," said his son, John Carter Cash.
"He loved to learn, and he loved to share."

Lived with JL Rivers one year
1st Home, at Saline Siding.

1st Son Roy born Sept 2 1921 in the parlor where they were married.

1st crop next year 1922

2nd Louise, March 1st 1924
Farming at Saline Side

3rd Jack Dom Nov 1st 1929
working public job -

4. J.R. Cash Feb 26 1932
on Buffalo Bills Birthday Mr. Cash Wanted to name the boy Buffalo Bill.

5. Reba. Jan 28 1934
Farming last crop in Cleveland County

March 24 1935 moved to Dyess.
Ray & 14 yr old Roy cleared 3acres raised 3acres cotton corn, beans sorghum -

8 or 10 acres in cultivation by 2nd year 1936. - Flood Jan 1937

LEFT Roy Cash, Johnny's eldest brother and the first artist among the Cash siblings, Memphis, Tennessee, ca. 1955. RIGHT Roy's daughters Jackie and Jan, Dyess, ca. mid-1950s

on any of us children." He went on to say that "in some ways my father is an enigma to me—the most interesting specter in my memories."

At the 2017 Johnny Cash Heritage Festival, historian and archivist Colin Woodward, formerly at the University of Arkansas at Little Rock (UALR) Center for Arkansas History and Culture, gave a presentation from his manuscript in progress, titled *Country Boy: The Roots of Johnny Cash*, which concentrated on the relationship between father and son. Noting that in the *Walk the Line* movie, Ray is depicted as the villain in the Johnny Cash story, Woodward argued that the history was far more difficult. Characterizing their connection as "often tense and troubled," he claimed that Johnny inherited his work ethic from his father and that his religion came as much from Ray as from Carrie.

There was another aspect of Ray that also impacted Johnny, and that was the genetics of addiction. In a 1956 letter to his first wife, Vivian Liberto, Johnny wrote that "my dad used to drink all the time," and in his autobiography he recalled the time that Ray came home drunk and killed the family's dog. Many years later, nearing the end of a life that had long been shaped by his own addictions, Cash said that "drug abuse runs through this family like a turkey through the corn."

High school friend A. J. Henson has a different recollection of Ray Cash. "I disagree that he was mean—he was strict," Henson said at the panel in Dyess. "It was a happy home. I spent many a night there. Four or five of us would sleep in one bed, but it was a happy family."

J.R. WAS ESPECIALLY CLOSE to his brother Jack, who was three years older; he described his bigger sibling as a "mentor and protector" who "gave me unconditional love." Jack planned to become a minister.

One Saturday morning in May of 1944, Jack was headed to the high school agriculture shop, where he had a job cutting oak trees into fence posts. J.R. was going fishing. Jack was stalling before leaving the house, telling his family that "I feel like something is going to happen." Carrie also experienced an odd sense of foreboding and urged him not to go to work; J.R. begged Jack to come with him to the fishing hole. But the teenager punched in for his shift, knowing that the Cashes needed the extra money.

J.R. realized that something serious had happened when his father suddenly showed up in the preacher's Model A Ford. Ray told J.R. that Jack had been hurt very badly, and when they got home, he took Jack's blood-soaked clothes out of a paper bag. One of the trees had gotten tangled in the table saw and dragged Jack into the blade, nearly cutting him in two. He held on for more than a week (A. J. Henson remembered Jack "suffering terrible") before dying on May 20, 1944, at the age of fifteen.

On his deathbed, Jack said that he had visions of heaven and asked if everyone around him could hear the sounds of the angels. "It's so wonderful," Cash recalled Jack saying as his final words, "and what a beautiful place that I'm going."

For the rest of his life, Cash would speak of the horrible guilt he felt over—and the constant inspiration he took from—this incident. "The memory of Jack's death," he wrote in *Man in Black*, "his vision of heaven, the effect his life had on the lives of others, and the image of Christ he projected have been more of an inspiration to me, I suppose, than anything else that has ever come to me through any man."

(Strangely, in a 1995 interview with journalist Nick Tosches, Cash floated an entirely different theory about Jack's death. "A neighbor went down to the shop with him that day and disappeared after the accident," he said, at least this one time. "I always thought of it as murder.")

Around the time of Jack's death, J.R. had made a new friend in Dyess Colony who lived near the fishing hole he had gone to on that fateful day. Jesse "Pete" Barnhill was an outsider, a squatter who was raised by his grandparents. In his high school yearbook photo, Barnhill looks a bit like an early rock and roller, with a hint of a sneer and dressed in black. He had polio, which "crippled his right leg and withered his right arm," as Cash wrote. He also had a guitar, a Gibson flattop, and J.R. had never been around someone with a guitar before.

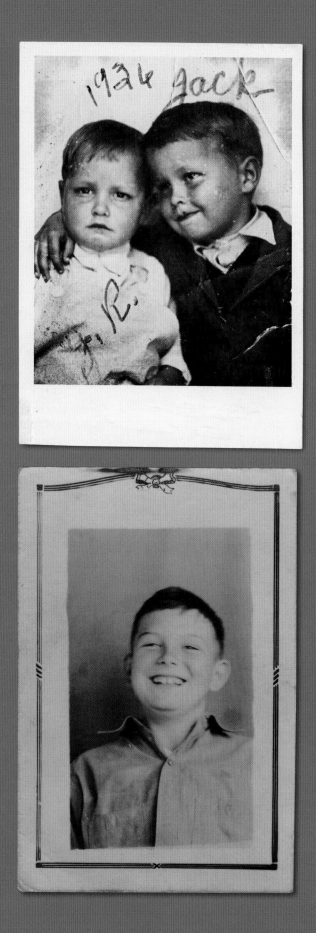

Jack Cash, 14, Dies After Sustaining Injuries At Dyess

Jack Cash, aged 14, son of Mr. and Mrs. Ray Cash of Dyess, formerly of Rison and Kingsland, died Saturday at the Dyess hospital. Young Cash's death followed injuries received about 10 days previously when he was cut severely about the body by a saw at the school shop.

Funeral services were conducted Sunday afternoon at the Dyess Baptist church by the Revs. Appling and Gallup. Burial was at Bassett cemetery.

Besides his parents, three brothers and three sisters survive.

"I started writing songs when I was about twelve," said Cash. "The death of my brother Jack had a lot to do with it." **CLOCKWISE FROM OPPOSITE TOP** Jack and Johnny, 1934. Jack's obituary, 1944. Jack's gravesite, Bassett, Arkansas. Jack, age ten, 1939

The two shared a love of music, an obsession with the sounds on the radio they were hearing from Memphis stations and on the *Grand Ole Opry*. Indeed, the radio had come to occupy an increasingly central place in Cash's life. (If you need an example of how different life was in rural Arkansas in the 1940s, consider this: Since the people had no electricity, the radios had to be battery powered. When the battery ran down, they would take it into town on their mule to get it recharged at the store.) Barnhill showed Cash how to play his first chords, and every afternoon they would meet up and sing tunes by Hank Snow, Ernest Tubb, and Jimmie Rodgers.

Until J.R. started making music, the oldest Cash son, Roy, had been considered the artist of the family, writing poetry, acting, and playing in a band, the Delta (or Dixie) Rhythm Ramblers, with four schoolmates; they had won a local talent contest and appeared on radio station KLCN in nearby Blytheville when J.R. was seven years old. But by the time his service in World War II ended Roy's performing dreams, his younger brother had picked up the torch.

J.R.'s classmates recall that he was always writing, and he had a poem to read every day in English class. A. J. Henson said that he "kinda liked being out front, always enjoyed performing…he would sing 'Trees' by Joyce Kilmer in assembly, and he wasn't nervous." At the Dyess event, Henson said that Cash wrote a poem for him to hand in as his own homework; it got an A grade. He then recited from memory: a story of a "top hand mount(ing) his trusty steed" and galloping across the plain. It ends: "He rode his trail until setting sun/Then rode a freight train back" (the train motif would run through so much of Johnny Cash's writing).

Soon, with Barnhill's guidance, he had enough basic skill on the guitar to begin setting his poems to music. "I started writing songs when I was about twelve," Cash said. "The death of my brother Jack had a lot to do with it."

This marriage of music and emotion, song and expression, was present from the very outset for Cash. His high school friends recalled a young man of remarkable sensitivity, attuned to his interior life in a way that stood in some relief against the masculine ideal of the time. A. J. Henson once said that Cash "went way down deep inside and brought up his feelings"; in Dyess, he added that his friend would "always think of and talk about things that were up in the air, that the rest of us didn't think about."

The fact that he stayed in school is either a tribute to his curiosity or to his family's indulgence. There were only thirteen in the graduating class of 1950. Everyone seems to remember Cash as a "nice country boy" (though Joyce Criswell, sister of a classmate, said he could be "kind of aggravating"). Henson spoke of a night when Cash was working the admission table at a basketball game, and when one kid didn't have the dime it cost to get in, J.R. went to the back door and snuck him inside.

Cash and Henson were part of a four-member "gang" of friends that also included J. E. Huff and Paul East. This crew did most everything together, walking everywhere until A.J.'s father bought a tractor. After this purchase,

Socializing back home in Dyess in 1950, the year
Cash (far right) enlisted in the military

A.J. would at times be able to take the tractor to pick up his friends and drive
to nearby towns such as Lepanto, to go to the movies and scope the girls—
"kind of exploring," said Henson. He added that it was difficult to imagine
J.R.'s later issues with addiction. "One of our other friends started drinking
and we said, 'If you do that, you can't run around with us.'"

Louise Nichols was Cash's first girlfriend. She indicated that his priorities were already becoming clear—one time he picked her up and said,
"You can carry my books, I gotta get my guitar!" He won the school talent
show singing a western number about horses and, just before graduation,
performed a version of "That Lucky Old Sun"—a song that had been a hit for
Frankie Laine, Louis Armstrong, and Frank Sinatra the previous year, and
that Cash himself would record exactly five decades later.

CASH'S THOUGHTS WERE TURNING to the larger world, and his ambitions clearly
exceeded anything Dyess had to offer, but what was he supposed to do? He

JULY 1954 *Studer* S.A.TEX.

A civilian again but not yet a star: with sister Louise
in Dyess in 1954, the year Cash was honorably
discharged from service

hopped on a bus in the neighboring town of Wilson and headed to Pontiac,
Michigan, where he took a job on an automobile assembly line. He lasted three
whole weeks. "The job itself was horrible," he wrote, "the accommodations no
better: a boardinghouse crammed tight with men who drank and cussed and
carried on more than my tender young country sensibilities could stand."

Returning to Arkansas, he saw that "there was nothing at home." The
farm had been worked to death and was producing a fraction of its former
yield. He tried a job at a local margarine plant and found himself "working
for low money in filth beyond belief and heat I'd never imagined possible."
And so, on July 7, 1950, he enlisted in the military—just after the Korean
War broke out —"the same way most other southern country boys did," he
said, "for lack of a better way out of the cotton fields." Cash chose the Air
Force, he once said, because "I just liked the image of flyin'."

Now renamed John R. Cash for purposes of official paperwork, he was
sent to San Antonio for basic training. He had asked Louise if she would
wait for him while he was away. He wrote her, sent pictures, and when he

Dyess High School senior portrait, taken at Brooks Air Force Base in Texas, 1950

Landsberger
December 10th

12 RSM

Dear Brother,
    Since it come a blizzard, and I can't go out,
I thought I might answer your letter that you wrote
the other day, Nov 2nd.
    And it did come a blizzard. I never saw any-
thing like it in my life. I was on my way back
from the PX this afternoon, minding my own business
and this big black cloud come up, like it was gonna
come one of them Arkansaw rains, but the sleet
and snow hit all at once, and I almost lost my
way before I got back. It's sure a cold, blue one,
right off the north sea. Seventeen degrees is
predicted for tonight, and colder tomorrow.
    Right now, I'm on a three-day pass, but I
think I'll wait till tomorrow to go anywhere,
due to the weather. I'm going down to Garmisch
in the Alps, and see if I can't break my neck
on a pair of skis. Things are pretty cheap
down there, so I hear, and plenty of free-
hearted little people.
    They changed my working schedule again
today. From now on, I only work six hours
a day, six days a week, with one three-day
pass per month. I'll be working from midnight
to six in the morning, the biggest part of the
time, which is the best shift for my job. The

only thing extra about this set-up is, I'll get
two hours per day of military training, and
they do mean military training. I'm gonna get
a little snow in my pants. I believe I'll like
it though, might need it sometime.
    Thursday, I went before the promotion board,
and I think I'll know tomorrow whether I made
it, or not. If I know the Air Force, I didn't.
They like to see a man sweat, then give it
to him the next month.
    The black market has gone to the dogs over
here. I can only get a little over double my
money for cigarettes and coffee. When I first
got here, I could get about 16 marks for cigs,
and now they've gone down to about 13 or 14.
    I guess you read about the big flood in Italy?
A lot of the boys here went down there to help
out, but I couldn't leave my job.
    Well, this is a good night for lots of things,
and I don't have a choice, so I'm gonna hit
the sack.
    Tell the wife and kids I said "hello" and,
Merry Christmas to all of you.

                        Love Brother
                            JR.

ABOVE A letter from Johnny (signing himself as JR) to his brother Roy, written from
Landsberg, Germany, 1953. OPPOSITE (top left) Cash's sister Joanne's husband
Bill Ingle, Joanne, Vivian, and Johnny in Dyess, 1955; Cash's snapshot from
Switzerland, 1951; Johnny at his Air Force training in San Antonio, 1953

came home on furlough, he brought her a compact because he didn't have money to buy a ring. But, she said, "he went his way and I went mine."

His way involved a dark-haired young woman named Vivian Liberto, whom he met at a skating rink in San Antonio and who—though they knew each other for barely three weeks before he shipped out—would be the one who really would wait for him when he was sent overseas. The hundreds of letters he wrote to Liberto during his service would make up a big chunk of her 2007 memoir, *I Walked the Line: My Life with Johnny.*

Cash was assigned to the 12th Radio Squadron Mobile of the US Air Force Security Service at Landsberg, Germany. He worked as a Morse code operator, intercepting Soviet Army transmissions—and he was good at it. "I was the ace," he wrote. "I was who they called when the hardest jobs came up." He copied the first news of Josef Stalin's death and located the signal when the first Soviet jet bomber flew from Moscow to Smolensk. (The listening equipment also enabled him to pick up a clear signal from Nashville's WSM, so that he could catch the weekly broadcast of the Grand Ole Opry.)

While he was in Germany, he was granted no home leave and only three telephone calls back to the States. But he went to London, Paris, and Barcelona. And for twenty deutsche marks, about five American dollars, he bought his first guitar. He formed his first band back at the base with two other airmen with guitars and a mandolin player. They called themselves the Landsberg Barbarians, and to pass the time they would "sit around together in the barracks and murder the country songs of the day and the gospel songs of our youth ... we were crude, but we had fun." Sometimes they would even try to perform in public. "We'd take our instruments to these honky-tonks and play until they threw us out or a fight started," he said.

With some of his savings, Cash bought a reel-to-reel tape recorder at the PX, and during down time, he would record the Barbarians and mess around with his own songs. One night, when he came off of his radio intercept post, he noticed that someone had been fiddling with the machine in his room. He slapped on one of the Barbarians' tapes and, when he pushed Play, what emerged was a series of weird noises and eerie drones.

He listened to the tape over and over, unable to figure out what was wrong. Eventually he realized that the tape had been threaded through the reels upside down, and he was hearing the recording playing backward (years before the Beatles and Jimi Hendrix started using such effects on purpose). The droning sound and mysterious chord changes, he later wrote, stayed with him and surfaced in the melody of one of his most defining songs—"I Walk the Line."

He also cut his first recording in a booth at the Munich railroad station for one deutsche mark; it was a version of Carl Smith's "Am I the One?" Carl Smith, interestingly enough, was married to June Carter at the time.

Cash was promoted to staff sergeant just weeks before his term of service was up, and the officers tried to persuade him to reenlist. But he had been

Johnny and fishing buddies in California, ca. 1962

too far from home for too long, and had been alarmed by the racism and violence he saw among the troops (though he had certainly joined in some of the beer drinking and hell raising himself). He was honorably discharged on July 3, 1954, and returned to Texas, where Vivian was waiting for him. But he needed to find a job if he was going to get married and start a family, and whereas the Landsberg Barbarians may have seemed just a convenient distraction, his dreams of making music were becoming more and more serious. The forces were pointing him toward one location, where a new musical revolution was brewing. John Cash was headed to Memphis.

HOME of the BLUES

Musical Influences

In 1992, Johnny Cash was inducted into the Rock and Roll Hall of Fame. There was, perhaps, an implied question hanging in the air at the event, since he was the first living artist associated primarily with country music to be voted into the institution. In his speech introducing Cash, Lyle Lovett pointed out the expansiveness of Cash's music. "He helped show the world what happens when rural sensibilities and values mix with an urban environment," Lovett said.

When Cash took the stage, he, too, emphasized the range of musical interests and influences he claimed. He thanked "some of my heroes . . . the Hanks, Hank Williams and Hank Snow, the Carter Family, the country folk from the hill country," and recalled the radio stations and record stores in Memphis where he was exposed to what was then called "race music" and other styles. "I heard some of my earliest heroes . . . Sister Rosetta Tharpe singing those great gospel songs.

"I bought some of the recordings by Alan Lomax, who did some field recordings back in the '30s and '40s," he continued. "He took his wire recorder into the alleys and the honky-tonks in Mississippi and South Carolina and Louisiana, and I listened to those by the hour, by the day, by the week and the month, and they influenced a lot of my writing—songs like 'Big River' and 'Get Rhythm.' Some of the earliest songs that I wrote were influenced by

....

"Some of my earliest heroes": Cash's inspirations included Sister Rosetta Tharpe, shown here performing in New York City, 1940.

people like Sister Rosetta Tharpe and by Pink Anderson and Blind Lemon Jefferson and some of the Carolina street singers."

Cash was explicit onstage that even he himself felt some doubt about whether his induction was entirely appropriate, and he was making a case that his work made sense next to the other inductees, which that year included the Jimi Hendrix Experience and the Yardbirds. Looking back over his own career, he mused that "maybe I was trying to make sure that I belonged here tonight," "make you see that I might possibly actually belong in the Rock and Roll Hall of Fame."

At least as far back as 1968, though—just a few months after launching a new magazine called *Rolling Stone*—Jann Wenner took stock of recent country music and wrote that "Johnny Cash, more than any other contemporary performer, is meaningful in a rock and roll context," going on to compare him to Bob Dylan and Otis Redding. From his early recordings, which were somewhat awkwardly placed alongside his Sun Records labelmates in the rockabilly category, to his final days, when he

LEFT Jimmie Rodgers, the "Singing Brakeman," ca. 1930. RIGHT Alan Lomax and Jerome Weisner of the Archive of American Folk Song talking outside the Library of Congress, ca. 1930

was seen as a badass forerunner of punk and even hip-hop, Cash never fit easily into any single genre. It's a reflection not just of his own curiosity and catholic tastes, but also of the unique moment in which he came of age.

Music was part of Cash's heritage. John L. Rivers, Carrie Cash's father, was a farmer who also served as a music teacher and song leader in his church. Carrie inherited her father's love of music and played the piano in the Baptist church in Dyess (though she herself was a Methodist).

When Cash first connected with Rick Rubin in the 1990s and the producer asked him to just start playing any songs he wanted to, among his first selections were some of the hymns he had grown up with, which his mother had taught him on her Sears, Roebuck–catalogue guitar. These sessions were later collected and released in 2004 as *My Mother's Hymn Book*, which Cash called "my favorite album I've ever made."

The songs were literally taken from a book of Carrie's, *Heavenly Highway Hymns*; Cash had held on to it for all those years ("it's kind of dog-eared and ragged, a little bit like I am," he said). In one day, he sat down and cranked through the ones he loved—"he knew all those songs by heart," said his friend and engineer David Ferguson—and they recorded twenty-some of the hymns, fifteen of which made up the record.

He initially set out to be a gospel singer, but church music wasn't all that young J. R. Cash

was listening to. Thanks to the magic of the radio, he was able to tune in to a wide range of sounds, from Roy Acuff, Eddy Arnold, and Ernest Tubb to Bing Crosby and the Andrews Sisters. He heard country and pop, gospel and blues. Every day during his lunch break from the cotton fields, he tried to catch Smilin' Eddie Hill's *High Noon Roundup* on WMPS, which presented the rootsier styles of the Louvin Brothers or the Lonesome Valley Trio (he was even able to visit the studio when he was fourteen years old). He listened to stations originating from New Orleans, Cincinnati, and Chicago.

"Radio was my lifeline," he told journalist Sylvie Simmons. "Radio was wonderful back then. It played everything . . . . Sometimes there might be a morning show where it was all country—or hillbilly, as they called it then—but otherwise the music was all mixed up. I was always the one in the family running the radio and getting the stations and finding the songs that I wanted to hear coming over the air, and I was the one singing along."

Performing in Dyess, Rosanne Cash introduced her song "50,000 Watts" by paying tribute to the radio that sat in an exalted place in her father's boyhood home. "What he must have felt coming across radio waves," she marveled. "We are changed by what we hear—this community of us who are married to the radio."

Towering over the competition, of course, was country music's most hallowed institution, the Grand Ole Opry, whose broadcast on WSM

defined the genre to the world at large thanks to a national hookup through NBC every Saturday night. The Opry (which remains the longest-running radio broadcast in US history) was founded in 1925 as a one-hour "barn dance," and membership is considered the greatest honor that can be bestowed on a country artist.

Cash would go on to have a contentious relationship with the Opry, but as a young southern boy, it loomed impossibly large over the culture. The Dyess High senior class even went on a field trip to Nashville to see the Opry's home at the Ryman Auditorium, "the mother church of country music."

His father told him he was wasting his time spending his free hours in front of the radio. "You're getting sucked in by all them people," he recalled Ray telling him. "That's going to keep you from making a living." But Carrie encouraged J.R.'s musical interests, even taking in laundry to pick up extra money to pay for singing lessons. Those didn't last long, though; halfway through his third lesson, the young teacher stopped him and asked him to sing something of his own choosing. Cash, unaccompanied, sang a Hank Williams song, and when he finished, she told him, "Don't ever take voice lessons again. Don't let me or anyone else change the way you sing."

Soon after, his voice broke, and his mother stopped him when she heard him singing around the house. "When I was seventeen years old," he said, "and my mother heard me sing the first time after my voice had dropped, she said 'God's hand is on you, you're going to be a well-known singer.' . . . I knew it myself."

Keep on the sunny side: the Carter Family, Nashville, ca. 1960. Left to right: June, Anita, Helen, and Mother Maybelle (seated)

"A Standard Of Comparison"

"Little children should I tell you tales
"Of trains and how their whistles blew
I tell you now lest I forget
It all was inspired by Hank Snow"

"I didnt ask Hank Snow where he got the lyrics for ~~his version~~ his version of Wabash Cannonball I never heard them before but long ago I decided that the way Hank Snow sings it is the way it ought to be when it comes to a train song.

I feel that what I have to say concerning my relationship with Hank Snows music might have some historical importance in Country music.

It was through the appreciation of the artistry of Hank Snow that I learned to appreciate the music of Jimmie Rodgers Still it is Hank Snow who remains for me a standard of comparison for any country artist.

As the age of the steam engine was coming to an end, the sound of Hank Snow came along to take you back anytime you like to the whiny rails of yesterday, to the hobo jungles where many a man was secretly happy, because he was doing the thing his heart longed to do; to ramble and see this great land of ours and to taste of the wild side of life on the sidetracks

Often when I tire of noise and light
And want to find a quiet place and go
A memory ticket to pleasant places
Is a song of the railroad by Hank Snow"

Cash's handwritten draft of liner notes for Hank Snow's LP *Tracks & Trains*, 1971

OF COURSE, THE STYLE that Johnny Cash would forever be associated with is country music, which raises the question of what exactly that category means. Critics, historians, and fans have argued over the definition of country music for as long as the term has existed, and there is probably no other genre that struggles constantly, perpetually, with the issue of what does and doesn't belong, what is or isn't country.

"A definition of country music is tough to corral, in any precise sense, without strangling the life right out of it," wrote David Cantwell and Bill Friskics-Warren in *Heartaches by the Number*. "This isn't to say that the music doesn't have certain defining features, such as its rural, southern, working-class roots, or a penchant for certain stringed instruments or harmony patterns . . . . [but] more than anything else, it's the tradition the people making records perceive themselves working out of, or the roots or influences they acknowledge, or just the affinities they display, that make their records country."

This is the tension at the heart of country music: how far can the literal connection to tradition be stretched to incorporate different sounds, instruments, and attitudes and still be accepted under the "country" umbrella? Historian Charles Wolfe wrote that before modern country splintered into numerous subgenres (alt-country, country rock, retro country), "it was a home of a large number of performers who shared a range of values and beliefs about the music, and who shared a common body of tradition and history." He called this strict sense of common ground a "great unifying, nourishing stream." Nick Tosches countered, though, that "from its inception, country and western was as mongrelized a style as any on earth."

Johnny Cash straddles both sides—all sides—of this never-ending debate. He was clearly rooted in the founding principles of country music; figures like the Carter Family and Jimmie Rodgers, themes of home and faith, images of farms and trains were present in his songs for his entire career. Yet the breadth of his musical interests always allowed other elements—folk songs, pop strings, rock rhythms—to find their way in when he was so inclined. Most significantly, Cash never really seemed to care whether anyone thought that his music was sufficiently country or not.

As he often said, one of his favorite singers and biggest inspirations was Sister Rosetta Tharpe, whose own unprecedented and groundbreaking career is instructive. Sister Rosetta, who grew up about ninety miles from Dyess, became famous in 1938 with a record called "Rock Me." She was a star through the 1940s—a black woman singing gospel music wearing a long, white, sequined dress and high heels, with an electric guitar slung around her neck. Her 1945 recording "Strange Things Happening Every Day" (which Cash later covered, one of several songs associated with Tharpe that he cut) has been credited as the first gospel song to cross over to the "race" charts—reaching Number 2 and helping set the stage for rock and roll.

Blurring the line between the sacred and secular worlds, she performed her music of "light" in the "darkness" of nightclubs and concert halls, and pushed spiritual music into the mainstream. In 1951, twenty-five thousand fans paid to attend her onstage wedding at Griffith Stadium in Washington, DC. Sister Rosetta was the first person to put a fourteen-year-old boy named "Little Richard" Penniman on a stage, and she became a model for Elvis Presley, Carl Perkins, and Jerry Lee Lewis.

So when Cash shouted Tharpe out in his Rock and Roll Hall of Fame speech (she herself was finally inducted in 2018, an honor that was long overdue), it was an indication of his musical inclusivity. He may have long ago stopped worrying about how a pure country audience received him, but he still knew that his own inspirations transcended boundaries and easy classifications.

The music of the years before Elvis Presley recorded "That's All Right Mama" in 1954 and opened up the rock and roll floodgates is generally written off as harmless pop pabulum. But a closer look at what actually dominated the radio during that time not surprisingly tells a more complicated story. In 1950, the year Cash graduated from high school, the annual chart had plenty of Bing Crosby, Patti Page, and Perry Como, but the biggest hit single was Gordon Jenkins and the Weavers' version of Lead Belly's folk lament, "Goodnight Irene." Number 2, in an era of near-complete pop segregation, was musical polymath Nat King Cole's "Mona Lisa." And Red Foley had one of the year's top hits with "Chattanoogie Shoe Shine Boy." The year before, almost unbelievably, Fats Domino had already had a million-selling hit with "The Fat Man."

During his formative years, then, Cash was able to soak up music from many sources and styles. Country music was where he came from, but it was never all he was. It's fitting that he included Alan Lomax in his thanks at the Hall of Fame, since in his early years, Cash had begun a musical expedition of his own, and he would spend the rest of his days searching out songs that moved him, regardless of genre.

In 1987, he even expressed his admiration for the heavy metal bands that his son was listening to, singling out Iron Maiden, Metallica, Motorhead, and Twisted Sister. "They were fabulous," Cash said, "just knocked me out." (Tipper Gore and the Parents Music Resource Center were just around then leading efforts to censor lyrics in pop music, and Cash made his displeasure known about their work—"How presumptuous people are my age to think that they're finally going to do something toward raisin' their kids right by censoring three minutes of what they hear in a day's dialogue.")

It was the same open-minded attitude that Cash had in 2001 when I spoke to him for the *Spin* magazine "Top 40" issue, naming the year's most vital artists. He had recently released *Solitary Man*, the third of the "American Recordings" series, and the *Spin* editors had placed him on the list in between no less than Pearl Jam and Destiny's Child. Over the telephone from his home in Jamaica, he didn't flinch when I asked him about Eminem, the most controversial figure in music at that moment.

"More power to him," Cash said. "If he's making the records he wants to make and people like them, then that's what it's all about."

3 GET RHYTHM

THIS PAGE Cash onstage with Luther Perkins (left) and Marshall Grant (right), ca. 1958. "Unlike Presley," wrote esteemed critic Ralph J. Gleason, "there are no bumps and grinds in his routine."

PREVIOUS Cash performing at a press party, February 1959, before he became "The Man in Black"

1955–1958

On August 7, 1954, one month after his discharge, John and Vivian were married at St. Ann's Roman Catholic Church in San Antonio. The ceremony was performed by her uncle, Father Vincent Liberto.

But they weren't staying in Texas. "Ever since that Sears Roebuck radio came into our house, Memphis had been the center of the world in my head," he wrote, "the one place where people didn't have to spend their lives sweating bare survival out of a few acres of dirt, where you could sing on the radio."

His older brother Roy had already moved to the city and hooked him up with a friend at the police department. It didn't seem the right fit for John, so the police chief suggested he go see if Home Equipment Company was hiring. Another introduction from Roy also proved fruitful, when he connected his brother with a pair of fellow mechanics at the auto shop where he worked—Luther Perkins and Marshall Grant, who played guitar and bass.

Soon John had a job as an appliance salesman (at which he claimed to be a total failure, with an extremely patient boss) and a group to play music with. He also had access to the explosion of music happening around Memphis at the time, from the rhythm and blues booming out of the clubs on Beale Street to the Home of the Blues record store to Dewey Phillips's *Red Hot and Blue* show on WHBQ—the leading edge of mixing white and black music together, playing anything that rocked, whether it was hillbilly, rhythm and blues, pop, or gospel. Moving to Memphis from the rural South,

"The whole world will know Johnny Cash," Elvis Presley once said. Here Cash poses for a publicity shot, ca. 1957.

Speer
MEMPHIS

Sun Records founder Sam Phillips poses for a portrait
with Cash in Memphis. Phillips is handing Cash a framed
record of "I Walk the Line" (released May 1, 1956) to
commemorate a milestone in album sales.

B. B. King once said, was like moving to Paris; it was a cosmopolitan, diverse
(if still decisively segregated), modern city.

John saw Elvis Presley play on a flatbed truck at the opening of a drug-
store when the kid had only one single out and performed those same two
songs over and over; the two singers met for the first time when John went
up to him after the show to say how much he liked his music.

Plugged into all of this activity was a wild-eyed genius named Sam Phillips (no relation to Dewey), who had opened the Memphis Recording Service
and the Sun Records label at 706 Union Avenue. Phillips, obsessed with
recording technology, had made a business out of documenting weddings,
funerals, and family events around town, and he was convinced that there
was an entire universe of musical talent that was not being represented by
the existing record business.

He recorded such giants as Howlin' Wolf and B. B. King at Sun, and a song
that is often considered the very first rock and roll record, 1951's "Rocket
88" by Jackie Brenston and his Delta Cats (a band actually led by nineteen-
year-old Ike Turner). But he also had hits with songs like "Just Walkin' in
the Rain" by the Prisonaires—actual prisoners who were escorted by armed
guard from the Tennessee State Penitentiary in Nashville to a session with
Phillips. The producer's vision was nothing less than a radical democrati-
zation of who could make music, of the very possibilities for art.

Onstage in 1963, with bassist Marshall Grant, drummer
W. S. "Fluke" Holland, and guitarist Luther Perkins

Cash, Perkins, and Grant gave their first public performance at a North
Memphis church. They didn't own any real "stage" clothes, so they wore
black shirts and blue jeans as a uniform—and since the show went over
well enough, wearing black onstage became a lifelong practice for Cash and,
eventually, his moniker, too. Encouraged by the reception, he started driving
around to the small towns outside Memphis, pitching his little group to local
theater managers and setting up appearances. They played a gospel-based
set, including the favorite of Cash's original compositions, "Belshazzar."

He eventually worked up the nerve to approach Sam Phillips and take
his shot at making records. He tried four or five times over the phone, presenting himself first as a gospel singer and then as a country singer, but
he got nowhere. Finally, he camped out at the front door of Sun Studio one

Contract Blank

AMERICAN FEDERATION OF MUSICIANS

OF THE UNITED STATES AND CANADA

(HEREIN CALLED "FEDERATION")

LOCAL NUMBER_____

THIS CONTRACT for the personal services of musicians, made this __16__ day of __December__ 19__55__

between the undersigned employer (hereinafter called the employer) and_____musicians (hereinafter called
employees) represented by the undersigned representative.   (Including Leaders)

WITNESSETH, That the employer employs the personal services of the employees, as musicians severally, and the employees severally, through

their representative, agree to render collectively to the employer services as musicians in the orchestra under the leadership of_____

_____Johnny Cash & Band_____, according to the following terms and conditions:

Name and Address of Place of Engagement____Big "D" Jamboree, Dallas, Texas._____

Date(s) of employment_____Saturday, January 7, 1956._____

Hours of employment_____Big D 8 till 10:45 and two appearances at the Round Up Club of___

____18 minutes duration each, one before 11:30 and one before 12:30_____

Type of engagement (specify whether dance, stage show, banquet, etc.)_____Stage show._____

The employer is hereby given an option to extend this agreement for a period of_____XXXX_____weeks beyond the original term thereof.

Said option can be made effective only by written notice from the employer to the employees not later than_____XXXX_____days prior to the expiration of said original term that he claims and exercises said option.

PRICE AGREED UPON $__125.00_____
                                    (Terms and Amount)

This price includes expenses agreed to be reimbursed by the employer in accordance with the attached schedule, or a schedule to be furnished the
employer on or before the date of engagement.

To be paid_____Upon completion of engagement._____
                                    (Specify When Payments Are to Be Made)

ADDITIONAL TERMS AND CONDITIONS

The employer shall at all times have complete control of the services which the employees will render under the specifications of this contract. On behalf of the employer the Leader will distribute the amount received from the employer to the employees, including himself, as indicated on the opposite side of this contract, or in place thereof on separate memorandum supplied to the employer at or before the commencement of the employment hereunder and take and turn over to the employer receipts therefor from each employee, including himself. The amount paid to the Leader includes the cost of transportation, which will be reported by the Leader to the employer. The employer hereby authorizes the Leader on his behalf to replace any employee who by illness, absence, or for any other reason does not perform any or all of the services provided for under this contract. Upon request by the Federation or the Local in whose jurisdiction the employees shall perform hereunder, the employer either shall make advance payment hereunder or shall post an appropriate bond.

The agreement of the employees to perform is subject to proven detention by sickness, accidents, or accidents to means of transportation, riots, strikes, epidemics, acts of God, or any other legitimate conditions beyond the control of the employees.

All employees covered by this agreement must be members in good standing of the Federation. However, if the employment provided for hereunder is subject to the Labor-Management Relations Act, 1947, all employees, who are members of the Federation when their employment commences hereunder, shall be continued in such employment only so long as they continue such membership in good standing. All other employees covered by this agreement, on or before the thirtieth day following the commencement of their employment, or the renewal of this agreement, whichever is later, shall become and continue to be members in good standing of the Federation. The provisions of this paragraph shall not become effective unless and until permitted by applicable law.

To the extent permitted by applicable law, nothing in this contract shall ever be construed so as to interfere with any duty owing by any employee hereunder to the Federation pursuant to its Constitution, By-Laws, Rules, Regulations and Orders.

Any employees who are parties to or affected by this contract, whose services hereunder or covered hereby, are prevented, suspended or stopped by reason of any lawful strike, ban, unfair list order or requirement of the Federation, shall be free to accept and engage in other employment of the same or similar character, or otherwise, for other employers or persons without any restraint, hindrance, penalty, obligation or liability whatever, any other provisions of this contract to the contrary notwithstanding.

The Business Representative of the Local of the Federation in whose jurisdiction the employees shall perform hereunder shall have access to the place of performance (except to private residences) for the purpose of conferring with the employees.

The performances to be rendered pursuant to this agreement are not to be recorded, reproduced, or transmitted from the place of performance, in any manner or by any means whatsoever, in the absence of a specific written agreement between the employer and the Federation relating to and permitting such recording, reproduction, or transmission.

The employer represents that there does not exist against him, in favor of any member of the Federation, any claim of any kind arising out of musical services rendered for any such employer. No member of the Federation will be required to perform any provisions of this contract or to render any services for said employer as long as any such claim is unsatisfied or unpaid, in whole or in part.

The employer in signing this contract himself, or having same signed by a representative, acknowledges his (her or their) authority to do so and hereby assumes liability for the amount stated herein.

To the extent permitted by applicable law, there are incorporated into and made part of this agreement, as though fully set forth herein, all of the By-Laws, Rules and Regulations of the Federation, and of any Local of the Federation in whose jurisdiction services are to be performed hereunder insofar as they do not conflict with those of the Federation.

Name of Employer____Ed McLemore_____   Accepted by Employer____[signature] Ed McLemore____

____Johnny Hicks_____   By Ed Watt

Street Address____Sportatorium_____   Accepted____John R. Cash____
                                                                              (Orchestra Leader)

City____Dallas_____ State____Texas____   Address_____

Phone____Sterling 4374_____   By_____
                                                                              (Representatives of Employees)

If this contract is made by a licensed booking agent, there must be inserted on the reverse side of the contract the name, address and telephone number of the collecting agent of the local union in whose jurisdiction the engagement is to be performed.

9-15-54 FORM B-2 Printed in U.S.A. ⬦ 44

in Va 56

OPPOSITE Cash's contract for the January 1956 Big
D Jamboree and two additional club sets in Dallas.
ABOVE The road goes on forever: Cash's snapshot of a
Virginia highway, taken on tour in 1956

Cash with Luther Perkins (left) and Marshall Grant (right), 1955. Cash recalled of his producer Sam Phillips that he "had to be a genius to get anything out of that conglomeration."

morning, waiting for Phillips to arrive. When the producer showed up, Cash said, "Mr. Phillips, sir, if you listen to me, you'll be glad you did," and his confidence was enough to get him inside.

On his own, Cash banged out selections he'd been practicing with his group, but Phillips insisted that he had no interest in recording gospel because there was no market for it. Cash tried classic country material by Hank Snow and Jimmie Rodgers, but Phillips kept asking whether Cash had any songs of his own. He mentioned a song he had started working on in Germany called "Hey Porter"—a story of a passenger on a train trip home to Tennessee that tapped into the feelings of missing home and the South that he felt overseas. After he sang it, Phillips told him to come back the next day with his band, and they'd try to make a record.

"Nobody I'd heard sounded like him," Phillips later said, which from him was perhaps the greatest compliment he could offer. "Even if you didn't like that voice, it got your attention."

When Cash returned to the studio for an informal audition with his band, he apologized for their limitations. The trio—augmented by steel guitar player Red Kernodle (another mechanic from the auto shop where Perkins and Grant worked)—was a nervous wreck. After they ran through three or four songs, Kernodle simply packed up his instrument and went home, saying "This music business is not for me"; Luther Perkins lay his right hand on the strings to mute them as he played, and in the absence of a drummer, Cash slipped wax paper between the frets and strings to create a snare-drum effect. "Phillips had to be a genius to get anything out of that conglomeration," Cash would tell biographer Robert Hilburn.

After a few takes, the producer got a version of "Hey Porter" that he was satisfied with, and he stunned the musicians by announcing that he wanted to put it out as a single. Of course, that meant another song was required for the b-side, so Cash had a homework assignment. Several weeks later, he called with the news that he had a contender; "Cry! Cry! Cry!" met Phillips's standards, but it still took no fewer than thirty-five takes to get the recording he wanted. Perkins was struggling with the guitar break Cash had asked for, until eventually they decided to scrap it and just stick with the chordal playing. What came to be known as Cash's basic "boom-chicka-boom" sound had been solidified.

"Hey Porter" was released on June 21, 1955, credited to "Johnny Cash and the Tennessee Two" (Phillips had renamed Johnny to sound more youthful, while in fact none of the three musicians was from Tennessee), a month after he and Vivian had welcomed their first child, daughter Rosanne. The single didn't make much noise, but enough DJs flipped the record over to the b-side that "Cry! Cry! Cry!" climbed to Number 14 on the country charts and sold more than 100,000 copies. When Cash returned to the Sun Studio in July, he cut four new songs—"So Doggone Lonesome" (inspired by Ernest Tubb), "Luther Played the Boogie" (a comic tribute to Perkins's distinctively rudimentary guitar style), "Mean Eyed Cat," and the first of his defining, signature compositions, "Folsom Prison Blues."

He had written the song when he was still stationed in Landsberg, inspired by the movie *Inside the Walls of Folsom Prison*. The melody and many of the words were pilfered from "Crescent City Blues" by Gordon Jenkins; later, when the song became popular following the *Live at Folsom Prison* album, Jenkins brought a lawsuit that resulted in Cash paying a settlement of approximately $75,000.

One thing that he hadn't borrowed, though, was the line that would become the best known, most quoted of his career: "I shot a man in Reno, just to watch him die." Cash said that he came up with these infamous words when "I sat with my pen in my hand, trying to think up the worst reason a person could have for killing another person, and that's what came to mind."

Phillips, meanwhile, was refining his production of Cash. He recognized that his use of tape delay—or "slapback" echo—was perfectly suited

Cash playing with Luther Perkins, Japan, 1962. "Even if you didn't like his voice, he got your attention," producer Sam Phillips once said of Cash.

ABOVE Cash signs autographs, ca. 1959. "Some artists go dry for a while," Cash's manager, Lou Robin, once said. "But there were always so many options for him." **OPPOSITE, CLOCKWISE FROM TOP LEFT** Snapshot of Cash taken by a fan in the United Kingdom, May 1956, Dave Hetzer and Cash in Biloxi, Mississippi, late 1950s, Cash signs autographs for fans, March 1958, Cash at a promotional appearance on a radio show, 1958

MAR 58

to the spare, serious tone of the singer's delivery. "Sam Phillips was a man of genuine vision," Cash wrote. "In my case he saw something nobody else had seen, and I hadn't even realized myself." Though Phillips was a technology buff, his spirit (and his ears) were moved by passion rather than precision. "He'd much rather have soul, fire, and heat than technical perfection," as Cash put it.

A week after this productive session, Cash made his first major concert appearance, opening for Elvis at the Overton Park Shell in Memphis on August 5, 1955. He made an immediate impression on Presley; June Carter Cash would recall that when she and her sister Anita were on tour opening for Elvis, he said to her that "Cash don't have to move a muscle, he just sings and stands there. . . . The whole world will know Johnny Cash." (The admiration was certainly mutual—Cash wrote that "every show I did with Elvis, I never missed the chance to stand in the wings and watch.") A 1957 clip of Cash in white shirt and jacket on Tex Ritter's *Ranch Party* television show, performing "Get Rhythm," a song he wrote with Elvis in mind, sounds strong and reveals a confidence and surety, though hardly challenges Presley's riveting on-camera dynamism.

The two-sided single of "Folsom" and "Lonesome" hit Number 4 on the charts, and it was time for Cash, Perkins, and Grant to hit the road, setting out on a circuit of regional one-nighters. Driving from show to show, grinding out the same brief set night after night, it was an exciting but demanding time. To get through the long drives and late hours, Cash (like most of his touring cohorts) started taking speed, which would later cascade into full-blown addiction. He recalled the first examples of out-of-control behavior—"I chopped a new doorway through the wall between my motel room and Marshall Grant's with a fire ax"—and recognized the toll that the road was taking on his relationship to Vivian and Rosanne. "My first marriage is especially tough to speak about," he wrote.

As with many of the emerging rockabilly artists and new-school country singers, the base of operations for Cash was a syndicated radio broadcast out of Shreveport known as the *Louisiana Hayride*. Broadcasting at 50,000 watts from KWKH on Saturday nights, the *Hayride* was one of dozens of such programs scattered across America in the wake of World War II. In contrast to its establishment rival the Grand Ole Opry, though, the *Hayride* was willing to take a chance on unknowns, and it was a key platform for Elvis and for Hank Williams, whose alcoholism and erratic behavior were too scandalous for the Opry.

The *Hayride*, which aired in front of a studio audience of around 2,000 at Shreveport's Municipal Auditorium, offered both a radio show and a branded touring package that traveled around the South for performances in between the Saturday night broadcasts. Cash loved the *Hayride* for its sense of community and creative integrity, and participated in the show off and on for almost eight years. "It's everything good happening at once,"

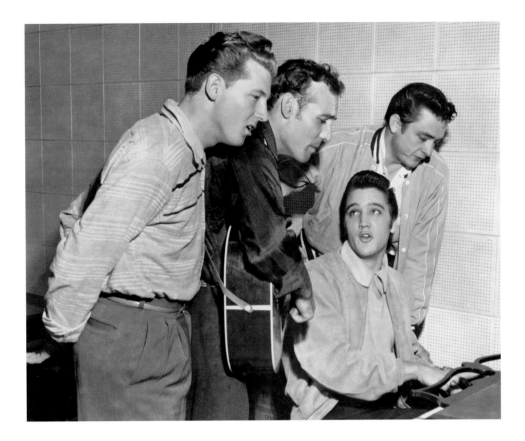

Rock and roll's most legendary jam session: the
"Million Dollar Quartet" summit of Jerry Lee Lewis,
Carl Perkins, Elvis Presley, and Johnny Cash at
Sun Studios, Memphis, December 4, 1956

he said, "being wanted, being appreciated, doing what I love, basking in a
great big family, playing music with my friends."

He was also growing close to the other artists signed to Sun. When he
met Carl Perkins, he said it was "like meeting my own brother," and they
became "friends for life." Following a show in Odessa, Texas, a young singer
named Roy Orbison shyly sidled up to Cash and asked for his advice about
approaching Sam Phillips for an audition. When Orbison first telephoned
Sun, Phillips said, "Tell Johnny Cash that he doesn't run Sun Records," and
hung up the phone. But after Orbison signed with the label, he and Cash
went on to become best friends.

When Cash got back to the studio in the spring of 1956, he brought in
the tune that would take him to the top—a song he had written the night
after his first *Hayride* appearance on November 13, 1955. With its eerie chord
progression based on the backwards tape sound he heard back in Germany,
and the singer ominously humming to himself between verses, "I Walk the
Line" was the sound of a man pledging fidelity even as he grappled with its
challenges. When he sang "I find it very, very easy to be true," it was apparent

TOP *Hot and Blue Guitar*, the first album Cash recorded, Sun Records, 1957. BOTTOM Poster for a Cash performance at the Hollywood Bowl, 1962

that he most certainly did not. He's singing to Vivian, of course, but he is also singing to himself, as a reminder, an affirmation, almost a dare.

In "I Walk the Line," wrote Bill Friskics-Warren, Cash is "confessing just how desperately he wants to unite the disparate strands of his gloriously conflicted self in hope of subduing the beast within." When Lyle Lovett inducted Cash into the Rock and Roll Hall of Fame, he said that the song was "more like air and like water than like a song that someone, some man, sat down and actually wrote, and sang."

Elvis Presley had recently left Sun for the major-label world of RCA Records, and Phillips used the money from that deal to help promote "I Walk the Line." The song hit Number One on the country charts and even crossed over to the pop Top 20. Bob Neal, Presley's former manager, was now handling Cash's career. And one dream was seemingly fulfilled when the Grand Ole Opry came calling.

But his Opry debut on July 7, 1956, did not feel like a triumph. In his autobiography he wrote, "Some people were suspicious of me since I was one of those rockabillies from Memphis." Though he spent two years as part of the Opry cast, later he described his reception more bluntly when he spoke to Rolling Stone's Steve Pond. At the Opry, he said, they called him "the same thing they were calling Elvis—'white nigger.'"

Journalists struggled with how to characterize young Johnny Cash. The Sun affiliation indicated that he should be lumped in with blues singers and rockabillies, but clearly his sound was something different. In a profile in the Nashville Banner, Ben A. Green—after noting that Carl Smith introduced Cash onstage as "the brightest rising star in country music of America"— quoted Cash as saying that "the fact [that] some of the songs have [a] definite rhythm beat does not make them rock and roll songs." Ralph J. Gleason, the preeminent pop music writer in the country, pointed out in the San Francisco Chronicle that "unlike Presley, there are no bumps and grinds in his routine."

ON DECEMBER 4, 1956, Elvis was home in Memphis and stopped by the Sun Studio. Carl Perkins was there for a recording session, and Jerry Lee Lewis—the label's latest acquisition and someone Cash had not heard or met before—was set to add the piano parts. Cash might have been in the room to watch his friend Perkins record; or he might have come by later in the day; or the Sun staff, sensing the promotional opportunity, might have gone out and found him. However it happened, the tapes rolled and, as the foursome sang their way through a slate of gospel songs, the "Million Dollar Quartet" was captured for posterity. Positioned farthest from the microphone, and singing higher than usual to harmonize with Presley, Cash's voice is barely audible on the recordings, but the image of the session is etched into rock and roll history.

Cash continued to record classics at 706 Union Avenue. His writing and Phillips's production merged to create a sound with unparalleled emotional punch. "The spare music framed the isolation in Cash's voice," wrote journalist Mikal Gilmore. In 1957, he became the first artist on Sun to release a long-playing album, *Johnny Cash with His Hot and Blue Guitar*.

The Sun recordings are taut, grimly elegant tales of a world where "just around the corner there's heartache." Elvis's rockabilly was expansive and free; Cash injected a bleaker strain of country history into rock—brooding, constricted, tense, stoic. Cash's songs are drenched in fatalism. "I don't like it, but I guess things happen that way," Cash sings without a shred of self-pity. In the lyrics of "Folsom Prison Blues," he acknowledges that "I know I can't be free," but he offers no apologies. The precise, detailed imagery of masterpieces like "Big River," matched by the stark guitar-and-bass accompaniment of the Tennessee Two, remains astonishing, and the influence of these recordings cannot be overestimated—they are the songs which directly inspired artists like John Mellencamp and Bruce Springsteen.

"Cash's was the stuff of unadulterated tragedy brought on by death, disaster, or loss of freedom," wrote Michael Streissguth. "[His voice] expressed an authority and seriousness, rarely if ever heard in country music."

At some point, Sun—largely in the person of renegade producer and engineer "Cowboy" Jack Clement, whom Phillips had brought on board—felt it was necessary to augment Cash's sound. On 1957's "Ballad of a Teenage Queen," Clement marred Cash's arrangement with a screeching soprano, superfluous instrumentation, and a lame backup chorus. The juvenile sentiment, too, was at odds with the gravity and maturity of Cash's usual presentation. It was a Number One hit, though, as well as his biggest pop song yet, reaching Number 14, and it proved to be the harbinger of the many overproduced Johnny Cash records to come.

Cash was becoming a national figure. Neal signed a deal for the singer to make ten appearances on *The Jackie Gleason Show* on CBS; he envisioned his client following Elvis's path to Hollywood, and taking on what he described as "John Wayne/Gary Cooper-type" roles.

Cash had become Sun's most consistently selling and prolific artist, but he was beginning to feel constrained by his contract with the small, independent label. Phillips was now concentrating his promotion on his latest breakout star, Jerry Lee Lewis. Cash wanted to record a gospel album, which Phillips had no interest in; and the company was still paying him a three percent royalty on his records, rather than the then-standard rate of five percent. Meantime, the Cashes' second daughter, Kathy, was born in 1956.

He was approached by Don Law at Columbia Records about joining their roster when his Sun contract expired. Law indicated that Columbia was open to the idea of Cash pursuing more creative projects, like the gospel record—they were looking at him as a career artist, not just someone living from hit to hit. He decided to make the move, but he didn't tell Phillips at first. He went on a recording tear and cut nearly a third of his entire Sun catalogue in the last three months of his contract—material that the label continued to release over the next several years.

Laughing with GRAMMY-winning country star Johnny
Horton outside the post office in Kingsland, Arkansas, 1959

"My feelings about Sam Phillips are still mixed," Cash wrote. "I'm not sure he treated me properly in a financial sense." Still, he always recognized the producer's genius and dryly observed, "If there hadn't been a Sam Phillips, I might still be working in a cotton field."

It had been a whirlwind few years for Johnny Cash. He came to Memphis a newlywed, just a few weeks out of the military, with no job and a dream of making music. Now he had three children, a Number One record, a long string of concert and television appearances, a simmering drug habit, and a new contract with a major record label.

In the summer of 1959, Cash, Vivian, Rosanne, Kathy, and newborn daughter Cindy left Tennessee and moved to Los Angeles, into a home that had belonged to another celebrity named Johnny—a rising television star named Johnny Carson. It was time to take yet another chance.

I GUESS THINGS HAPPEN THAT WAY

4

THIS PAGE Vivian, Johnny, and (left to right) daughters Kathy and Rosanne, with daughter Cindy on Johnny's lap, at home in Hendersonville, Tennessee, January 1960

PREVIOUS "I knew that I could do different kinds of things": Cash in a promotional photo, 1957

1959–1967

n the 1961 film *Five Minutes to Live*, Johnny Cash plays Johnny Cabot, a bank robber and violent sociopath hiding out in the California suburbs. Recruited for a large-scale heist, he poses as a door-to-door guitar teacher, under which cover he is able to both take the bank president's wife hostage and conveniently have his instrument in hand to sing the title song. "I guess you gals is all alike when ol' Johnny steps on your starter," he sneers.

When the financing for *Five Minutes to Live* (also released under the title *Door-to-Door Maniac*) ran out during the shoot, Cash put up $20,000 of his own money. That was probably a sign that he was not going to be following his friend Elvis into instant Hollywood stardom, though later in his career, he actually put together a credible run of roles in TV series and movies.

Moving his still-growing family west (fourth daughter Tara was born in 1961) was more difficult than he had anticipated. "I didn't really belong [in California]," he said. "I never really felt at home there."

But he immediately set to work exploring the creative freedom that his deal with Columbia Records promised. "I knew that I could do different kinds of things with a larger label," he said. First up was recording the gospel album that Don Law had approved, 1959's *Hymns by Johnny Cash*. The music wasn't all traditional, however—he wrote or cowrote about half of the songs, and the arrangements added only backup vocals to the spare Sun style.

Nor did the album signal a move away from the commercial marketplace. *Hymns* was recorded concurrently with *The Fabulous Johnny Cash*, which

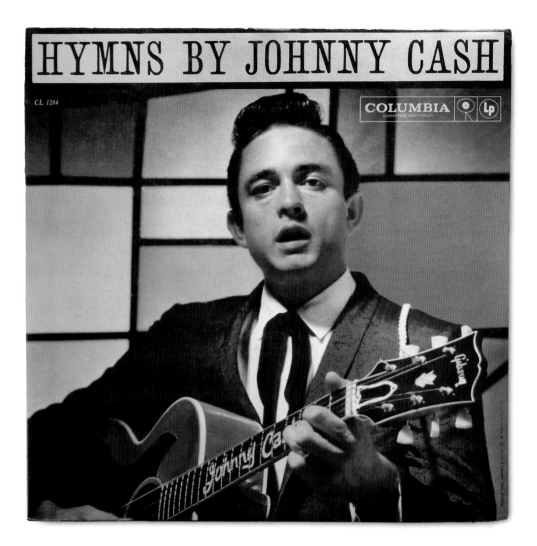

Front of Cash's *Hymns* album, released in 1959
on Columbia Records

included the classics "I Still Miss Someone" and "Don't Take Your Guns to Town" and was his first album to reach the Top 20.

More significant was *Ride This Train*, released in 1960, the first in a long list of "concept albums." Cash's fascination with trains had surfaced in his very first singles—"Hey Porter" and "Folsom Prison Blues"—but now he had something more extensive in mind.

"When I was a boy, the trains ran by my house," he later said in the *Ridin' the Rails* television special, "and they carried with them the promise that somewhere down the tracks, anything would be possible." So when it came time to record his eighth album, he came up with an idea that would take it beyond the usual collection of songs. "I must have had a country opera in my mind without knowing it," he said.

The album is billed on the cover as "a stirring travelogue of America," with Cash providing spoken narration before each of the twelve songs, for

Cash listens to playback with engineers at Columbia
Studios in Nashville, ca. 1963. Cash used the studio
to push forward the way that albums were constructed.

context. In several cases, he assumes the voice of such historical characters as John Wesley Hardin, and describes various destinations around the
United States visited by train.

Interestingly, the subject matter of the songs themselves is not necessarily trains or railroads. The album is less literal, and more complicated—the
point is the way Cash assembles and connects the songs. "*Ride This Train* is
not so much about trains," wrote Greg Kot, "as it is about the people and events
one might see from the windows of a passenger car rolling back through
time." Though it didn't chart, it opened up new potential for Cash's use of
the album format.

The next year, he also began working with a new manager, Saul Holiff,
who was thinking bigger about Cash's career. A former concert promoter in
Canada, Holiff "pushed me to take my show, and my career, to another level,"
wrote Cash. Instead of only ballrooms and dance halls, he started booking
Cash into larger venues and into markets beyond the United States. Holiff

Master tape of 1960's *Ride This Train*, with handwritten track list on the case. "I must have had a country opera in my mind without knowing it," Cash said.

managed Cash into the 1970s; their sometimes-stormy relationship was the subject of a documentary by Holiff's son Jonathan titled *My Father and the Man in Black*.

For all the things his new manager was able to accomplish, perhaps the most significant was a single concert date, December 9, 1961. He had booked Cash to play the Big D Jamboree in Dallas on a bill with the Carter Family, where Cash reencountered June Carter. They had met backstage at the Grand Ole Opry, when they were both married to other people. Powerful sparks had flown.

In 1962, the Carter Family joined Cash's tour, and the temptation continued to grow. "She was a vivacious, exuberant, funny, happy girl," wrote Cash about his early impressions of June, "as talented and spirited and strong-willed as they come, bringing out the best in me."

June later said that, though she had divorced Carl Smith in 1956, "it wasn't a convenient time" to fall in love. "I was miserable, and it all came to me: I'm falling in love with somebody I have no right to fall in love with." Encouraged by legendary director Elia Kazan (*A Streetcar Named Desire*, *On the Waterfront*, *East of Eden*), she moved to New York to attend the Actors Studio, but when Kazan stopped making movies—he made only three films after 1963—her opportunity stalled.

Meanwhile, Cash's recording career wasn't exactly stumbling but seemed as if perhaps it had plateaued. He hadn't had a single reach the Top 20 since leaving Sun; such songs as "Tennessee Flat-Top Box" and "In the Jailhouse Now" kept up his presence on country radio, but despite the ambitions of his albums, pop success was drifting farther out of reach.

On May 10, 1962, he fulfilled a dream by headlining a sold-out show at Carnegie Hall. But he was agitated, nervous, and his voice was shot. His drug use was increasing, and he showed up late for the gig and in no shape to perform. Cash also badly miscalculated in planning the show as a tribute to Jimmie Rodgers, because when he took the stage in Rodgers's signature brakeman's outfit, it was clear the audience had no idea what he was doing.

The show was a disaster, and he left the Carnegie Hall stage in what he described as a "deep depression." Afterward, he consoled himself by heading downtown with a folk singer friend to hear some music at Greenwich Village's The Bitter End. Performing was Native American protest balladeer Peter La Farge, whose songs made a great impression on Cash and whom he befriended.

With great irony—or perhaps none at all—it wasn't just a song by June Carter that put him back in the game, it was a song specifically written about the torment of their illicit attraction. Merle Kilgore was also part of the 1962 tour package; his composition "Wolverton Mountain," covered by Claude King, spent nine weeks at Number One on the country charts as the tour rolled along. Merle and June, who lived a few blocks apart in Nashville, often wrote together.

At one of their sessions, June noted an underlined phrase in a book of Elizabethan poetry that had been owned by her uncle, A. P. Carter: "Love is like a burning ring of fire." It hit close to home, given her current circumstances, and she started a new song. "There is no way to be in that kind of hell, no way to extinguish a flame that burns, burns, burns," she wrote.

Later that day, Anita Carter called her sister from the studio, saying that she needed one final song to finish her new album. June and Merle knocked out the rest of the song, and Anita quickly recorded it under the title "(Love's) Ring of Fire." Appearing on her 1963 album *Folk Songs Old and New*, the track was featured as a "spotlight pick" by *Billboard*, but it didn't make the charts.

Cash claimed that he had a dream in which he heard the song accompanied by "Mexican horns." He told Anita that he would wait a few months and see if her version took off, and if it didn't hit, he would record it himself. On March 25, 1963, he called in his old friend from Sun days, Jack Clement, to arrange the mariachi trumpets, and recorded "Ring of Fire" with Mother Maybelle, Helen, June, and Anita Carter singing harmony.

In her memoir, Vivian Liberto told a different version of the song's origin. She claimed that several months after Anita's version had been released, her then-husband told her that he had written the song while drunk and high on a fishing trip with Kilgore, and that the title referred to a part of the female anatomy. Cash's friend Curly Lewis, who was also fishing with them that day, backed up this story.

Cash and the "Tennessee Two" (neither of whom was actually from Tennessee), bassist Marshall Grant (far left) and guitarist Luther Perkins (left), performing with Hank Snow (far right) at the Grand Ole Opry, Nashville, ca. 1950. "Some people were suspicious of me since I was one of those rockabillies from Memphis," Cash later recalled.

"To this day, it confounds me to hear the elaborate details June told of writing that song for Johnny," Liberto wrote. "She didn't write that song any more than I did." She added that Cash decided to give Carter cowriter status simply because "she needs the money." Kilgore always insisted, though, that he and June were the song's composers.

Regardless of its provenance, "Ring of Fire" and its exotic-sounding tale of lust and "wild desire" became a huge hit for Cash. It reached Number One on the country charts in 1963 and stayed there for seven weeks, and got to Number 17 on the pop charts. It became a defining song in his career—

CARNEGIE HALL

(Order of Appearance & Maximum Time Allotted Each Performer)

No

~~7:50~~ - Johnny Western - Introductory Remarks (in essence warm-up) in
brevity some of the reasons for this concert.

8:00 - JOHNNY WESTERN - ~~2 Songs~~   *1 Song*

8:07 - Introduction - Glaser Brothers - by Johnny Western

8:08 - TOMPALL & THE GLASER BROTHERS (maximum 15 min. stage work) → *4 Songs + Encore*

8:22 - Introduction - Gordon Terry - by Johnny Western ——

8:23 - GORDON TERRY (Maximum 15 min. stage work) → *3 Songs, incl Fiddle + Encore*

8:38 - Introduction - George Jones - by Johnny Western

8:39 - GEORGE JONES - (maximum 15 min. stage work) *- OK Encore*

J. Western Sings Ballad

8:54 - Introduction - Mac Wiseman - by Johnny Western

8:55 - MAC WISEMAN (maximum 15 min. stage work) *- OK - Encore*

9:10 - Introduction - Maybelle & Carters - by Johnny Western

9:11 - MOTHER MAYBELLE & THE CARTER FAMILY (maximum 15 min. stage work) → *20 m Encore*

9:26 - INTERMISSION (Tompall & Glasers, Mother Maybelle & Carters,
please stand by second half to do pre-arranged
numbers with Johnny.)

9:46 - Introduction - Johnny Cash - by Johnny Western → *OFF Stage*

9:47 - JOHNNY CASH & THE TENNESSEE ~~TWO TAILO ONE~~ *THREE*

Selections: → *1 hr - 20 min*

*Cannot be numbered
Just time me out*

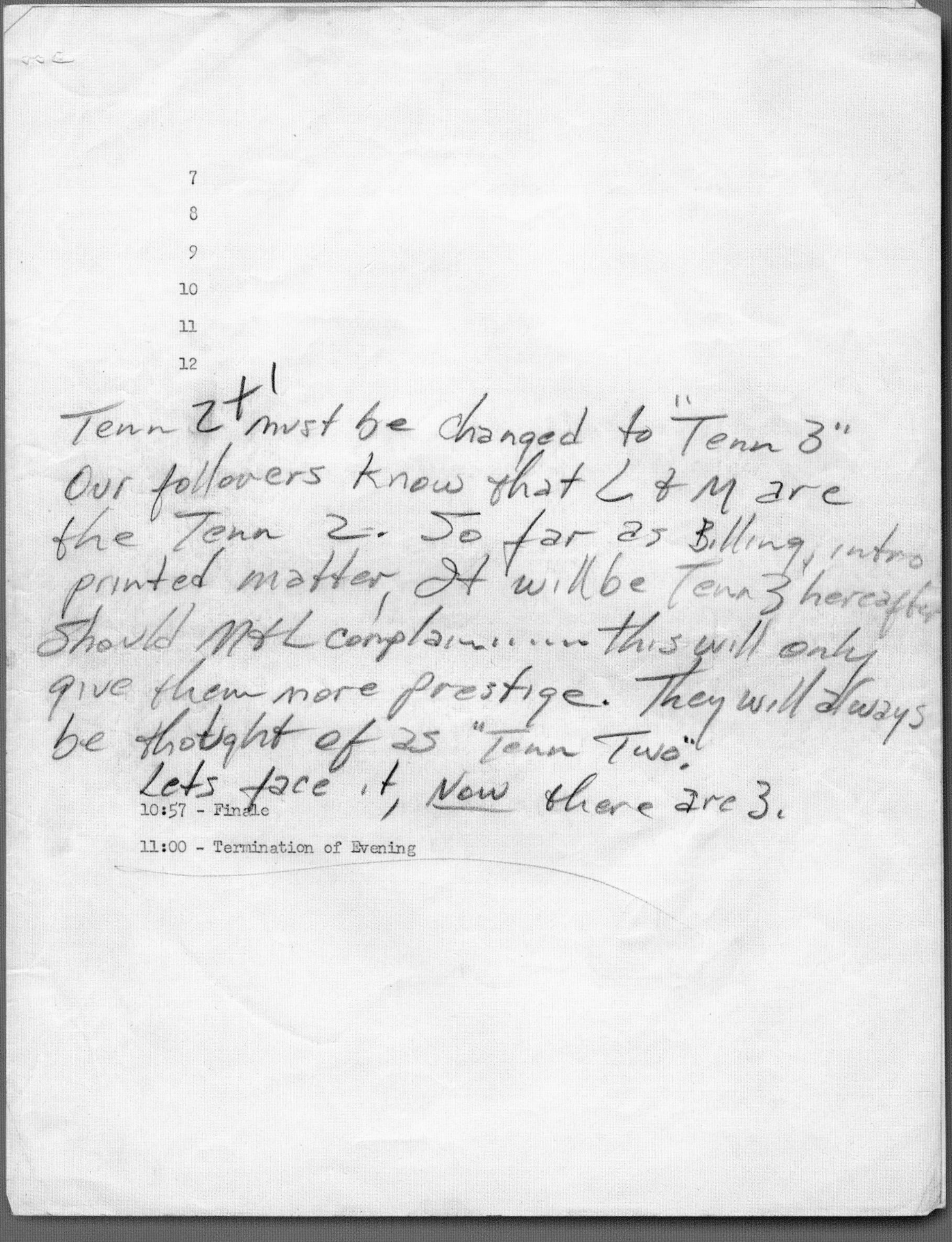

7

8

9

10

11

12

"Tenn 2"+1 must be changed to "Tenn 3"
Our followers know that L & M are
the Tenn 2. So far as Billing, intro
printed matter, It will be Tenn 3 hereafter.
Should M&L complain........ this will only
give them more prestige. They will always
be thought of as "Tenn Two".
Lets face it, Now there are 3.

10:57 - Finale

11:00 - Termination of Evening

Cash's handwritten notations on the lineup and billing for his ambitious
but ultimately disastrous debut at Carnegie Hall, May 10, 1962

inducted into the GRAMMY Hall of Fame; ranked at Number 87 on *Rolling Stone*'s 500 Greatest Songs of All Time; covered by the likes of Eric Burdon and the Animals, Social Distortion, Alan Jackson, and Frank Zappa.

Cash was becoming increasingly interested in the folk music boom of the early 1960s and, on visits to New York, was spending more time in the Greenwich Village clubs that were the focal point for the movement. While some looked at the folkies as shaggy, radical undesirables, Cash responded to the integrity and purpose of the music. His 1962 *Blood, Sweat and Tears* album was a step in the folk direction, assembling a collection of songs about the American working man that included "The Legend of John Henry's Hammer," "Casey Jones," "Chain Gang," and Harlan Howard's song "Busted," a single that hit the country charts as Ray Charles's version was concurrently climbing the pop charts.

In 1964, he took on one of the boldest projects of his career. *Bitter Tears: Ballads of the American Indians* was another concept album, this one focusing on the tragic history and unfair treatment of Native Americans in the United States. Inspired by a new sense of activism among the country's indigenous peoples and the topical songwriters he was hearing in the Village, he decided to address these issues head-on, stepping far outside the usual parameters of major-label country music.

Five of the songs were written by Peter La Farge, two were by Cash alone, and the final track, "The Vanishing Race," was credited to the great Johnny Horton ("The Battle of New Orleans," "North to Alaska"). Though by this time Cash's albums seen together risked seeming like a checklist of American themes, *Bitter Tears* was perhaps the most sophisticated and daring of the series. (In 2015, it was the subject of a PBS documentary, *We're Still Here: Johnny Cash's* Bitter Tears *Revisited*, accompanied by an album with such artists as Emmylou Harris, Steve Earle, and Kris Kristofferson rerecording *Bitter Tears'* songs.)

The record opened with La Farge's "As Long as the Grass Shall Grow," recounting the loss of Seneca Nation land in Pennsylvania and New York due to federal construction of the Kinzua Dam. La Farge's "Custer" mocked the popular veneration of General George Custer who, though often considered a military hero, was in fact overwhelmingly defeated, in part due to his own errors, by Lakota warriors at Little Big Horn.

The signature song of *Bitter Tears*, though, was "The Ballad of Ira Hayes," a La Farge composition about the young Marine who was part of the iconic flag-raising on Iwo Jima during World War II. The photo of the event made Hayes a celebrity, but he struggled after the war. He returned to his native Gila River Reservation in Arizona, where, in another case of loss to Native people, the government had built a dam that diverted critical water supply. Hayes died in 1955 of alcoholism and in poverty.

Bitter Tears reached Number 2 on the country charts and skimmed the Top 50 overall. "The Ballad of Ira Hayes" started out quickly on the singles

Greenwich Village–based folk musician and singer-songwriter
Peter La Farge poses for a portrait in New York City, August 1962.

chart, but six weeks later it was dropping. There was a sense that the story
was too dark, the theme too controversial for country radio, the statements
too shocking for an audience heavily invested in the myth of the American
cowboy. Cash refused to accept the backlash quietly.

He took out a full-page ad that appeared in the August 22, 1964, issue
of *Billboard*, challenging the resistance to the song. "D.J.'s, station managers,
owners, etc.—where are your guts?," he wrote. "I had to fight back when I
realized that so many stations are afraid of Ira Hayes. Just one question:
WHY???" He concluded the message with "'Ballad of Ira Hayes' is strong medicine....So is Rochester—Harlem—Birmingham and VietNam." He bought and
sent out more than a thousand copies of the single to radio stations across
America, and by September 19, the song had clawed its way to Number 3
on the country singles chart.

A few weeks after he completed the sessions for *Bitter Tears*, Cash
attended the Newport Folk Festival, where he met Bob Dylan for the first
time. He had become obsessed with the 1963 album *The Freewheelin' Bob
Dylan*, later saying that he thought Dylan was "the best hillbilly singer I'd

OPPOSITE An ad that Cash placed in *Billboard* magazine, August 22, 1964, challenging DJs to play his recording of "The Ballad of Ira Hayes," which describes the life of a Native American Marine who was among the famed flag raisers on Iwo Jima during World War II. ABOVE Johnny with daughters Rosanne, Tara, Cindy, and Kathy, Hendersonville, Tennessee, 1969

ever heard." Cash's eight-song set at Newport included a performance of Dylan's "Don't Think Twice, It's All Right" alongside "Ira Hayes," the inevitable "Folsom Prison Blues" and "I Walk the Line," and the traditional songs "Rock Island Line" and "Keep on the Sunny Side."

In 1964, social tensions in America had not risen to the fever pitch they would reach later in the decade, but the ease with which Cash crossed the lines between commercial country and folk protest was remarkable. After his Newport set, in a gesture like something from Arthurian legend, he presented Dylan with one of his guitars, sealing a friendship that would last the rest of his lifetime.

CREATIVELY, "RING OF FIRE" and *Bitter Tears* had given Cash some momentum. Offstage, though, his life was falling apart. He was tormented by his simmering love for June, knowing that when he was home with Vivian and the girls during his breaks from the road, he was torturing them all. "There was

Johnny Cash

It is an astounding experience, the power that touches everyone who walks around the gigantic statue of the W.W. II flag-raising based on that classic picture from Iwo Jima. There are 5 Marines and one Navy corpsman depicted in that bronze giant at Arlington national cemetery.

I "chilled" like that recently, then went to Columbia records and recorded "The Ballad of Ira Hayes."

D.J.'s—station managers—owners, etc., where are your <u>guts</u>?

(I know many of you "Top 40," "Top 50" or what-have you. So . . . a few of you can disregard this "protest" and that is what it is.)

I think that you do have "<u>guts</u>" . . . that you believe in something deep down.

I'm not afraid to sing the hard, bitter lines that the son of Oliver La Farge wrote.

(And pardon the dialect—mine is one of 500 or more in this land.)

Still . . . actual sales on Ballad of Ira Hayes are more than double the "Big Country Hit" sales average.

Classify me, categorize me—STIFLE me, but it won't work.

I am fighting no particular cause. If I did, it would soon make me a sluggard. For as time changes, I change.

This song is not of an unsung hero. The name Ira Hayes has been used and abused in every bar across the nation.

These lyrics, I realize, take us back to the truth—as written by his cousin, Peter La Farge (son of the late Oliver La Farge . . . author, and hard worker in the department of Indian Affairs, Washington, D. C., until 2 years ago.)

You're right! Teenage girls and Beatle record buyers don't want to hear this sad story of Ira Hayes—but who cries more easily, and who always go to sad movies to cry??? Teenage girls.

Some of you "Top Forty" D.J.'s went all out for this at first. Thanks anyway. Maybe the program director or station manager will reconsider.

This ad (go ahead and call it that) costs like hell. Would you, or those pulling the strings for you, go to the mike with a new approach? That is, listen again to the record?

Yes, I cut records to try for "sales." Another word we could use is "success."

Regardless of the trade charts—the categorizing, classifying and restrictions of air play, this is not a country song, not as it is being sold. It is a fine reason though for the <u>gutless</u> to give it thumbs down.

"Ballad of Ira Hayes" <u>is</u> strong medicine. So is Rochester—Harlem—Birmingham and VietNam.

In closing—at the Newport Folk Festival this month I visited with many, many "folk" singers—Peter, Paul & Mary, Theodore Bikel, Joan Baez, Bob Dylan (to drop a few names) and Pete Seeger.

I was given 20 minutes on their Saturday nite show (thanks to Mr. John Hammond, pioneer for Columbia by way of A/R).

The Ballad of Ira Hayes stole my part of the show. And we all know that the audience (of near 20,000) were not "country" or hillbillies. They were an intelligent cross-section of American youth—and middle age.

I've blown my horn now, just this once, then no more. Since I've said these things now, I find myself not caring if the record is programmed or not. I won't ask you to cram it down their throats.

But as an American who is almost a half-breed Cherokee-Mohawk (and who knows what else?)—I had to fight back when I realized that so many stations are afraid of "Ira Hayes."

Just one question: WHY???

Johnny Cash

Cash's address book, early 1960s, prominently
featuring the birthday of his first wife, Vivian. Note also
the listing for his high school friend A. J. Henson.

Trade ad, *Variety*, 1964, targeted at the folk music market

always a battle at home," he wrote, but said that because of Vivian's Catholic upbringing, "she'd die before she'd give me a divorce."

Rosanne described her father at the time as being "so wired you would almost break down in tears to be in the same room with him. He'd set fires. He seemed so miserable." In another interview, she said, "I saw my dad and I thought, 'This is just about the worst thing that could happen to someone.'"

It wasn't just the unrequited love for June Carter that was eating at Cash. He had also fallen deep into a drug habit, gobbling amphetamines at a ferocious pace. In his autobiography, he recalled his first encounters with drugs—at age eleven, when he was given morphine while he was in the hospital for a broken rib, and then when he started taking speed while he was on the road during the Sun years. "I took drugs because it made me feel good" was the simple explanation he once offered, but he also noted that the feeling "was never as great as the first time."

Though it is often part of the Johnny Cash mystique that he was able to relate so well to prisoners and stake so much of his career on his Folsom and San Quentin concerts because he had served time in jail himself, he was always careful to point out the very limited experience he had behind bars. During his drug-abusing years in the 1960s, he found himself in jail "seven different times in seven different places, over a seven-year period." His drug-related offenses ranged from the ridiculous to the alarming.

On May 11, 1965, he was arrested in Starkville, Mississippi, following a performance at Mississippi State University. Cash was charged with public drunkenness after being caught in a local resident's garden picking flowers.

He shared his cell that night with a fifteen-year-old named Smokey Evans. After kicking the wall so hard that he broke his toe, Cash took off his shoes and gave them to the boy, saying, "Here's a souvenir. I'm Johnny Cash."

He later wrote "Starkville City Jail" about the incident. In 1969, before singing the song to the inmates at San Quentin, he recounted the experience, to uproarious laughter.

"You wouldn't believe it, one night I got in jail in Starkville, Mississippi, for picking flowers. I was walking down the street . . . and uh, you know, going to get me some cigarettes or something. 'Bout two o'clock in the morning, after a show, I think it was. Anyway, I reached down and picked a dandelion here and a daisy there as I went along, and this car pulls up. He said, 'Get it the hell in here, boy, what are you doing?' I said, 'I'm just picking flowers.' Well, thirty-six dollars for picking flowers and a night in jail. You can't hardly win, can ya? No telling what they'd do if you pull an apple or something."

There is, in fact, no Starkville City Jail. Cash was actually kept in the Oktibbeha County Jail. In 2007, the city of Starkville symbolically pardoned him, in a ceremony that was part of the inaugural Johnny Cash Flower Pickin' Festival.

In June 1965, Cash's camper caught fire during a fishing trip with his nephew Damon Fielder in California's Los Padres National Forest. The resulting fire burned more than five hundred acres. Cash claimed that the blaze was caused by sparks from a defective exhaust system on his camper, but Fielder said that Cash started a fire to stay warm and, in his drugged condition, failed to notice the flames expanding. When the judge asked Cash why he did it, Cash flippantly replied, "I didn't do it, my truck did, and it's dead, so you can't question it."

The fire also drove off forty-nine of the refuge's fifty-three endangered condors; Cash's response was "I don't care about your damn yellow buzzards." The federal government sued him—he said that he was the only person ever sued by the government for starting a forest fire—and was awarded $125,172. Cash eventually settled the case and paid a fine of $82,000.

Cash's rapid downward spiral led to a more notorious incident less than four months later, in October, when he was stopped at the border in El Paso coming back into the country from Juárez, and 668 Dexedrine and 475 Equanil tablets were found in his guitar and suitcase. "I felt like the outlaw I had become," he said, "sitting in a taxicab on a hot, dirty back street behind a bar in Mexico waiting impatiently for the pusher to fill my order."

But when his case came before the judge, once again he sounded more petulant than repentant. "I am guilty of as many sins as the average person," he said, "but I don't say that I am guilty of any more than the average person." He received a suspended sentence and paid a small fine, but the image of Cash being led away in handcuffs was indelible—a badge of honor for his rebellious fans as much as a permanent strike against him with more conservative listeners.

He knew the depth to which he was sinking, the darkness that was descending on him. "I think it was the miserable streak in me," he later said. "Maybe I was afraid to face reality then. I wasn't very happy then. Maybe I was trying to find a spiritual satisfaction in drugs." And he was aware of the pain he was inflicting on his family. "My first wife put up with me for years after I was hooked," he said. "It was like I was living with a bunch of demons."

Vivian came to El Paso for the hearing, and an Associated Press shot of the couple on the courthouse steps ran in newspapers the next day. To some readers it appeared that Vivian—a dark-featured Italian-American woman who was rarely photographed—was black. The National States Rights Party, an Alabama white supremacist group, republished the photo in its newspaper, the *Thunderbolt*, attacking Cash with racist accusations: The money generated by his hits, it claimed, went "to scum like Johnny Cash to keep them supplied with dope and negro women."

Cash was harassed and boycotted by some southern fans, though the drug arrest led to more concert cancellations than the race-mixing rumors. "Johnny and I received death threats, and an already shameful situation was made infinitely worse," wrote Vivian. (Reports that Vivian was black continue to turn up on the internet to this day.)

Also in October, Cash made a disastrous return to the Grand Ole Opry stage. Faced with a faulty microphone stand, he flew into a rage, picked up the stand, and smashed the footlights out in front of horrified audience members.

"I don't know how bad they wanted me in the first place, but the night I broke all the lights on the stage with the microphone stand, they said they couldn't use me anymore," he said. "So I left and used that as an excuse to really get wild, and wound up in the hospital with my third time I broke my nose." Indeed, like the legendary Hank Williams before him, Cash's onstage fit earned him a ban from the Opry, though he would later be welcomed back.

He recalled his lowest points without sentimentality, apology, or pity. And he always assumed responsibility for his actions, no matter how dire. "My father could be incredibly self-destructive and in a lot of psychic pain," Rosanne

Cash (center), flanked by a bondsman and a US marshal as he is transferred from El Paso County Jail to the federal courthouse in El Paso, Texas, October 5, 1965. Cash was arrested at the International Airport in El Paso and charged with importing and concealing more than a thousand "pep" pills and tranquilizers. His bond was set at $1,500.

Cash once said, "and he would never, ever, ever blame anyone else—or purposely hurt someone, or take it out on someone. To me, that defines integrity."

On the road, June was trying to keep him alive, searching his room for pills, flushing any that she found down the toilet, hunting him down on nights when he disappeared from the bus or the hotel. In *Cash: The Autobiography*, he recalled the one night that she gave up on him and said she was leaving the tour. It was the mid-'60s, in the Four Seasons Hotel in Toronto.

"I was nothing but leather and bone," he wrote. "There was nothing in my blood but amphetamines; there was nothing in my heart but loneliness; there was nothing between me and my God but distance."

Still, he wasn't ready to stop. In the summer of 1966, Vivian finally consented to his wishes and filed for a divorce, but it would not be granted until the end of 1967. He moved to Nashville and fell in with a new batch of renegade singers and songwriters who were ready to match his chemical intake head-to-head.

He shared an apartment with Waylon Jennings. "Me and John were the world champions at pill-taking, but we each didn't let the other know that we knew it," Jennings wrote in his autobiography. "I hid my stash in the back of the air conditioner, while John kept his behind the television. He'd tear the place apart if he ran out. If we had started combining supplies and sources, we probably would've bottomed out and killed ourselves, feeding each other's habits."

In the 1997 biography *Go, Cat, Go!*, Carl Perkins told writer David McGee about going to visit Cash in the house he subsequently moved into in Hendersonville, about an hour outside of Nashville (soon adding the "House of Cash" museum and gift shop across the street). "He'd cook up the awfullest platter of that ugly-looking ham," said Perkins, Cash's dear friend from the Sun days who remained part of his touring show. "If there had been any furniture in the house, he'd of tore it all to pieces. Had one big ol' round bed upstairs, and that's what he had. Out there in that mansion by himself...he'd stay straight for a few dates and then he'd turn into that wild Indian again."

Kris Kristofferson told Nicholas Dawidoff about Cash's reputation when Kristofferson relocated to Nashville in the mid-'60s to try his hand at the music business. "When I first went to Nashville, he was skinny as a snake and just as impossible to predict," he said. "Everybody was afraid of him." And remember—these are Cash's friends talking about him. His recordings, meanwhile, were getting less and less relevant. In 1966, he put out the collection of novelty songs *Everybody Loves a Nut* ("The One on the Right Is on the Left," a cynical jab at musicians who took political stands, was actually a hit) and the perfunctory *Happiness Is You*, both quickly forgotten.

For his presentation at the 2017 Johnny Cash Heritage Festival, Cash historian Mark Stielper spoke about the events in the singer's life around October of 1967, a brief period of dramatic change. Just a few months earlier, he had released an album of duets called, somewhat astonishingly, *Carryin' On with Johnny Cash and June Carter*; we can only imagine what Vivian Liberto Cash made of this project (and its title). It included the steamy "Jackson," a Number 2 country hit that went on to win a GRAMMY. "We got married in a fever/Hotter than a pepper sprout," sang the still-not-married couple.

But he was flailing, his life in shambles, and he could see no way out. "I was a walking vision of death," he said. During those weeks, day after day, there were signs of his anguish. After a show in South Bend, Indiana, he wrote a letter pouring out his anger and despair. He drove by himself to rural Georgia, where he had some close friends in and around Lookout Mountain, hoping the escape would help. Returning to Hendersonville, he drove to a spot called Nickajack Cave, near the Tennessee River, just west of Chattanooga. There, he claimed, he crawled inside the cave, deeper and deeper, finally stopping in the dark, determined to wait there until he died.

But he had an epiphany while he was underground. "I was not in charge of my destiny," he realized, and he would die when God decided it was time, not when he did. He dragged himself back to the surface, first feeling air and then seeing light; when he emerged from the cave, his mother and June Carter were waiting there, having sensed that something was wrong and finding his parked Jeep. He determined then and there, he said, that he would clean himself up.

The Nickajack story is central to the Johnny Cash mythology. Country singer Gary Allan even wrote a song called "Nickajack Cave: Johnny Cash's Redemption" ("High above him shone a light, he never would forget/Then he heard a voice say, 'Johnny Cash, I ain't through with you yet'"). Further research, though, has indicated some problems with the tale as told. Robert Hilburn discovered that Nickajack Cave was in fact flooded during the fall of 1967, and entry would have been impossible. And, Stielper pointed out, there is no way that Cash, with his lifelong fear of snakes, would have willingly climbed down into the depths of that cave.

What had actually happened? "You had to take what he said with a grain of salt; he would say, 'Never let the truth get in the way of a good story,'" according to John Carter Cash. "So where was the cave? Was there a cave? I think there was, but it wasn't the same one he said. But does it matter?"

In any case, Cash did not get sober immediately. The next month, returning to Georgia, he got his Cadillac stuck in the mud, started walking through a rainstorm, and wound up on a woman's porch. She met him with a shotgun, he fell into her garden, and the local police, finding a bag of pills on him—and turning down a bribe to look the other way—took him to the town of Lafayette. Sheriff Ralph Jones generously released him after giving him a long talk, warning him about the danger of his behavior and wasted potential. (Cash later returned to Lafayette to play a benefit concert in gratitude, raising $75,000 for the high school.) Two months later, when he performed at Folsom Prison, he was still taking pills.

But the Nickajack story, whether Cash himself believed it or not, "dramatized the feelings of helplessness and recovery," writes Hilburn. Stielper gives the metaphorical impact of the legend even more power. "Whether he crawled into Nickajack to die is almost beside the point," he said in Dyess. "He saw nothing but blackness in his life, and he was given God's grace to see the light."

In a very short time, that despair would turn around, and Johnny Cash's life—public and private, creative and commercial, romantic and physical—would enter an entirely new phase.

The MAN in BLACK

Social Concerns

"He was willing and able to be the champion of people who didn't have one." That was how Kris Kristofferson characterized Cash after his friend and colleague's death. For all of his musical accomplishments and contributions, one thing that distinguishes Cash from many other great artists was his genuine sympathy with and understanding of the underdog, and his consistent use of his platform to give a voice to the voiceless, led not by dogma but by simple human decency.

He was also drawn to stories of rebels, outsiders, and long shots, and used the materials as themes for songs. This, Cash believed, was not a unique position for him to take, but placed him in a true American tradition. "Our heroes in song were, for the most part, anti-establishment," he once wrote. "We want to feel his pain, his loneliness, we want to be a part of that rebellion."

Some believed that this attitude tipped over into glamorizing the actions of criminals, but he pushed back against that interpretation of his own music, or of those who faced similar accusations throughout pop music history. "The biggest-selling song of the nineteenth century was a song about a bandit and an outlaw and a killer," he said to me in 2001. "It was called 'The Ballad of Jesse James.' And those themes have carried through up until now.

"I watched Elvis go through it—people saying, 'You're leading our children to hell!' I've been hearing it all my life. But I have yet to hear anyone take it seriously and actually shoot a man in Reno just because my song said so."

For the liner notes to box set *Love God Murder*—a collection released in 2000 with three discs, each of them dedicated to one of the three themes in the title—Quentin Tarantino contributed his thoughts on the "murder" group. He called them "poems to the criminal mentality," writing that "Cash sings tales of men trying to escape . . . but the one thing Cash never lets them escape is regret."

His own beliefs about crime and punishment manifested themselves most visibly, of course, in the concerts he played at prisons throughout his career. The public was made aware of these shows in the late 1960s, when he released the best-selling albums recorded at Folsom and San Quentin. But Cash had actually been playing for prisoners for many years at that point, and had performed at San Quentin as far back as 1958. And his concern went beyond just showing up for musical performances: In 1972, Cash testified at a US Senate judiciary subcommittee hearing on prison reform, offering his support for proposals to

Cash receives an honor from a tribal elder, St. Francis, South Dakota, 1968

"I just don't think prisons do any good": Johnny and June exiting the front gate of Kansas State Prison, ca. 1968

keep minors out of jail and to focus on rehabilitating inmates.

"I didn't go into it thinking about it as a 'crusade,'" he said. "I mean, I just don't think prisons do any good. They put 'em in there and just make 'em worse." He expressed his opinion about the prison system more succinctly to Robert Hilburn. "I don't know how much good drudgery does anybody," he said.

The most notable aspect of his prison concerts, in addition to the simple fact that he was prioritizing these appearances on his schedule, was the respect that he showed for the incarcerated. Merle Haggard, who was in the audience for one of the early San Quentin shows

while he was locked up after an arrest for robbery, clearly remembered Cash's onstage attitude.

"What stood out, even more than his music, was his demeanor," Haggard later said. "He was a bit cocky and a bit arrogant . . . it seemed like it didn't matter [to him] whether he was able to sing [well] or not." The Country Music Hall of Famer recalled the concert as something that "may have been the first ray of daylight I had seen in my entire life." (In another interview, though, he made sure to point out the limitations of Cash's identification with prisoners—"Johnny Cash understands what it's like to be in prison," he said, "but he doesn't *know*.")

In 1973, Albert Nussbaum—once on the FBI's Ten Most Wanted list for bank robbery—wrote an account of Cash's appearance at Leavenworth for Charleston, West Virginia's *Sunday Gazette Mail*. He focused mostly on the effect that Cash had simply by acknowledging the humanity of those behind bars. "We came because we care," Nussbaum quoted Cash telling the crowd. "We care. We really do. If there's ever anything I can do for you all, let me know somehow, and I'll do it."

The convict described how Cash would "handle [his] guitar as though it were a weapon," and how the jail population's connection to "Folsom Prison Blues" was so strong that most of them were overcome. "It captured our own feelings so exactly that our roar of approval completely drowned out the music," wrote Nussbaum.

The other cause that Cash pursued over the years was his commitment to Native Americans. As far back as 1957, he had written a song called "Old Apache Squaw," after which he "forgot the so-called Indian protest for a while. But nobody else seemed to speak up with any volume of voice."

The advent of the folk movement, though, lit a fire under Cash to speak his mind on the treatment of Native Americans . "Johnny wanted more than the hillbilly jangle," said Peter La Farge, the Native American songwriter who would become a key collaborator during this period. "He was hungry for the depth and truth heard only in the folk field."

This led, most notably, to the *Bitter Tears: Ballads of the American Indian* album in 1964, and his battle for acceptance of the La Farge-composed single, "The Ballad of Ira Hayes." The project faced genuine opposition from Cash's label and from the country music establishment, with one journalist even urging him to leave the Country Music Association, on the grounds that "you and your crowd are just too intelligent to associate with plain country folks, country artists, and country DJs."

The hard-fought success he ultimately achieved with "Ira Hayes" was hardly the end of his involvement with Native American issues. In 1966, in recognition of his advocacy, Cash was adopted by the Seneca Nation's Turtle Clan. In 1968, he performed a benefit concert at the Rosebud Reservation, close to the historical landmark of the massacre at Wounded Knee, to raise money to help build a school.

The 1969 documentary *Johnny Cash: The Man, His World, His Music* includes footage of him singing "Ira Hayes" at the Rosebud Reservation's St. Francis Mission school. The elders bless him in a ceremony, reciting "Oh, great spirit, watch him and watch over him," and he recounts his feelings while visiting Wounded Knee—"such a mystical air hung over the place."

In 1970, Cash recorded a reading of John G. Burnett's 1890 essay on Cherokee removal for the Historical Landmarks Association in Nashville, and on *The Johnny Cash Show*, he told numerous stories of the mistreatment of Native Americans , both in song and through short films, such as the history of the Trail of Tears. As late as the 1980s, he played at California's D–Q University, one of the first tribal colleges in the United States.

Where did this passion for the Native American cause come from? Cash sometimes toyed with reporters by referring to his own Cherokee heritage, but there was no truth to that tale. As a student of history, proud of the research he did on his thematically based albums, he clearly saw the injustices that had been done to his country's indigenous people. Maybe his own upbringing on a farm, and especially in a cooperative community, gave him a different relationship to those who had been displaced from their land, from the resources and opportunities to thrive by their own labor. As with his work on behalf of prisoners, maybe Cash just liked the idea of being able to speak up for those who he felt were misunderstood and misrepresented to the general public.

He was always adamant that his social efforts were neither political nor partisan. "I don't think it would be fair for me to campaign for a presidential candidate and try to influence people that way," he told Patrick Carr in 1976. "That's important stuff and big stuff and I don't think I've got a right to exercise any such control over the people." In fact, for all his opinions and stances, Cash never voted in an election.

He was proud of performing in the White House at the invitation of Richard Nixon in 1970, though he would not accommodate the president's request that he sing two satirical country hits (Merle Haggard's "Okie from Muskogee" and Guy Drake's "Welfare Cadillac") that happened to demean hippies and welfare recipients; Cash insisted, perhaps not wanting to be seen as insulting the President, that his refusal was because the ask was put in too late for him to learn the songs. In his introductory remarks, Nixon joked that one thing he'd learned about the singer was that you didn't

Chatting with inmates at Cummins Prison Farm, Arkansas, 1969. "What stood out even more than his music was his demeanor," said Merle Haggard of Cash's prison performances.

tell him what to sing. A few years later, Cash registered his outrage over the Watergate affair, saying it "made me sick and ashamed."

Like many Americans, Cash's opinions of the war in Vietnam evolved as the fighting dragged on. Initially reluctant to criticize the government or the military, by the conflict's later years he was more forthright. The situation in Vietnam, he said, "just made me sick. I'm not supporting that war or any other war." Though it would be tough to call Johnny Cash a pacifist, he did say this: "The only good thing that ever came from a war is a song, and that's a hell of a way to have to get your songs." By the mid-'70s, these were hardly radical words, but they were not being heard from most veterans, southerners, or country music singers.

Cash attempted to summarize all of his philosophies in one of his most self-defining and self-mythologizing songs, 1971's "Man in Black." Here, he turns his fashion choices into

a metaphor for his worldview. Though he has often explained that he wore black clothes onstage out of superstition, or for their simplicity, or because they could go longer without washing and still look clean, now the color took on symbolic meaning as a protest against poverty, war, prisons, ageism—all "the ones who are held back."

The song solidified his standing as a beacon of social justice, an outlaw with a conscience, a rock and roll Robin Hood who would inspire future generations even if they had only passing knowledge of his music. Rosanne Cash also believed that the song offered something more personal about her father, beyond just securing Cash's reputation as a spokesman for the ignored and oppressed.

"There's so many levels to it," she told *Mojo* magazine in 2008. "One is saying, 'I'm wearing this symbol for the downtrodden and the poor.' The other was much more subtle to me:

it reflected the sadness, the convulsions, just that mythic dark night of the soul that he went through so many times."

Because ultimately, what Johnny Cash and his commitment to these various causes comes down to is a concept that has become so prominent in recent years—it's the idea of empathy. His truest concern, in his songs and in his life, often revolved around the sense of understanding someone else's condition, trying to feel their plight. Though he survived so much that he was able to identify with those who were struggling, the truth is that his hope for connection predates his own battles with addiction or fidelity or loss. He was the Man in Black long before he identified himself as such.

"Dad appealed to so many people in so many ways in so many different places," says John Carter Cash, "because he truly was a champion for everyman, he honestly cared. He could put himself in a place of humility, to know what it felt like to be a prisoner. Whether that was a fantasy or an illusion, those people *knew* it, and you could not tell them otherwise."

When we spoke in 2002, Cash told me that the songs on his new album were "talking about the pain and the hurt, and the human spirit that overcomes—and all of us have gone through the hard times and know what we speak of when we speak of these things."

He had put it another way in a 1975 interview with Larry Linderman for *Penthouse* magazine. Linderman asked Cash what he thought his songs communicated to people, and Cash spoke about reaching different audiences, trying to avoid being "put in a bag," and remembering that music belongs to everybody.

"I just think it's fascinating for a man to spread himself around," he said, "to walk through different doors, see different groups of people, and understand and feel what they react to. You learn a lot."

Johnny Cash and June Carter walk through the Folsom Prison yard on January 13, 1968—a historic day in music history. The two married shortly after that on March 1, 1968.

FLESH AND BLOOD

5

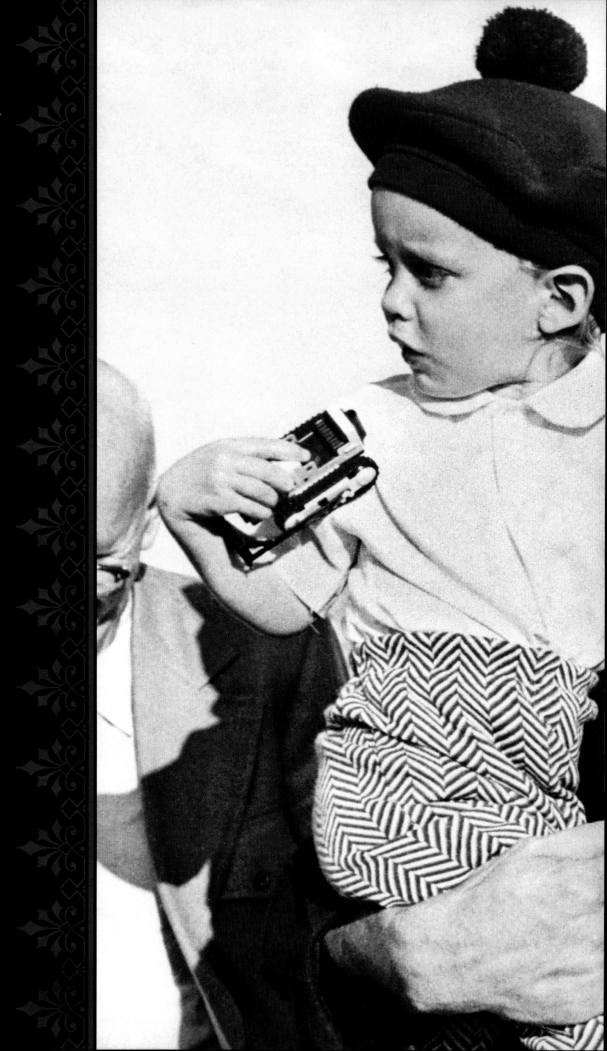

1968–1974

As the 1960s progressed, Johnny Cash's career was running out of steam. He continued to release albums that were devoted to exploring a specific theme in American music or history (*Johnny Cash Sings the Ballads of the True West*, *From Sea to Shining Sea*), but to mostly diminishing returns—the records didn't cross over to the pop charts, and *From Sea to Shining Sea* was his worst performance ever on the country charts.

Cash maintained that this period wasn't any kind of disaster. "The 1960s were probably my most productive time, creatively speaking," he wrote, adding that "I also disagree with the opinion that I didn't make good records in the 60s." He pointed to the extensive research he did for the concept albums and the voice he was giving to different communities.

Now that his divorce from Vivian had gone through, he was determined to get clean for June. He still stumbled—he crashed his tractor into Old Hickory Lake, behind his house in Hendersonville, but said that while he was underwater, he remembered the fourth verse of "How Great Thou Art." It was yet another sign that he needed to get it together. He went through a detox under the supervision of Dr. Nat Winston, who was the Tennessee commissioner of mental health and would later run for governor. According to Cash, Winston told him, "I don't think there is much chance for you. I've never known of anyone as far gone as you are to really whip it."

But June continued to hold out hope. She had been friendly with Hank Williams (in one of his only TV appearances, on *The Kate Smith Evening*

Cash at the Columbia Records Convention, Los Angeles, California, July 1959

Rehearsing with June at El Rancho Motel, Sacramento,
the night before the Folsom Prison concerts, 1968

Hour in 1952, he dedicated his performance of "Hey, Good Lookin'" to twenty-two-year-old June) and she said simply, "Hank had died and I didn't want John to die."

There had been some changes to the executive team at Columbia Records, and in 1967, Bob Johnston, who had produced some of Bob Dylan's most celebrated material, was put in charge of Cash's recordings. Cash saw this as an opportunity to pitch an idea that he had long dreamed of but the label had always refused—cutting an album live during one of his prison concerts. (In truth, there had been plans to record a 1965 show at Kansas State Reformatory, but the show was cancelled given Cash's condition at the time; after that the label wasn't willing to risk setting up a live recording of any kind.)

Johnston pounced on the idea, immediately picking up his phone and calling San Quentin. When he couldn't get through, he called Folsom Prison, the source of one of Cash's greatest hits, unaware that the singer had played there as recently as 1966. The warden was enthusiastic, and two performances were scheduled for January 13, 1968. Still, not everyone was convinced about the commercial viability of the project—"I told everybody it won't sell enough to pay for the expense of going out with the recording equipment," said Cash's drummer W. S. "Fluke" Holland.

Johnny and June checked into the El Rancho Motel in Sacramento, joined by the rest of the acts in the show—the Tennessee Three, the Statler Brothers, and Carl Perkins (who was now part of Cash's band in addition to playing a few of his own hits in the set; "I was never very comfortable having him standing behind me on stage, literally in my shadow," Cash wrote)—as well as Johnny's father; producer Johnston; and Reverend Floyd Gressett, the pastor of Avenue Community Church, where Cash sometimes attended services. Gressett also counseled inmates at Folsom and helped facilitate the concert.

The performers rehearsed until nearly midnight on the eve of the shows, allowing extra time to learn a new song, "Greystone Chapel." The spiritual about the grace of God was written by Folsom inmate Glen Sherley, who was doing five years to life for armed robbery. Sherley had given a cassette of the song to the prison's recreation director, who passed it on to Gressett, who in turn presented it to Cash. That evening, California governor Ronald Reagan, who was holding a fundraiser at the hotel, visited the band and offered his encouragement.

Cash arrived at Folsom early in the morning; the first show in the prison cafeteria was set for 9:40 a.m. He was told that conditions were a bit tense because two weeks earlier, some of the convicts had held a guard at knifepoint, and they had been warned that the show would be stopped if anyone so much as left his seat. He saw that armed guards were observing from ramps overhead. Cash was already nervous—and had downed a bunch of pills before leaving the motel.

Out of this tension, though, came one of the most storied performances in music history. His signature introduction—"Hello, I'm Johnny Cash"—was followed not by the usual whoops and screams, but by a dramatic silence from the audience of 1,000 who had been put on notice to behave and to "welcome him" only after he had spoken. He then opened, inevitably, with "Folsom Prison Blues." The eighteen songs that followed covered a remarkable, perfectly attuned emotional range—multiple songs focusing on prison life ("The Wall," "Green, Green Grass of Home," Shel Silverstein's comic execution countdown "25 Minutes to Go"), but also songs of despair ("Dark as a Dungeon," "Long Black Veil") and of low comedy ("Dirty Old Egg-Sucking Dog," "Flushed from the Bathroom of Your Heart").

He played up his outlaw side; "I just wanna tell ya that this show is being recorded for an album release on Columbia Records and you can't say 'hell' or 'shit' or anything like that," he smirked at one point. "To this assembly," wrote music critic Tom Moon of the *Folsom* album in *1,000 Recordings to Hear Before You Die*, "he's not a temporary escape from the drudgery of the pen, but a living symbol of the rebel road."

It was a set that demonstrated sympathy for the prisoners' circumstances, but also granted them respect and humanity. He was both sentimental and defiant. "Cash never lays anything on thick," wrote Moon. "He leaves room for the listener's own reckonings, and implies emotional undercurrents without stating them." This appearance, wrote Mikal Gilmore, secured the notion that "nobody else in popular music could match Cash for radical nerve or compassion."

Cash ended the show with "Greystone Chapel," to the delight of the audience. "Hope we do your song justice, Glen," he said to Sherley, who was seated in the front row. He shook Sherley's hand at the end of the song, then headed backstage, where the songwriting convict was brought to him for a few minutes of conversation. (He later brought Sherley with him when he testified in Congress on prison reform, and then made him part of the touring party, but Sherley displayed emotional troubles and committed suicide in 1978; Cash never mentions his name in the autobiography.)

Cash swapped out a few songs for the second set, which was recorded as a backup for the album, with two of the numbers he added ("Give My Love to Rose" and "I Got Stripes," yet another prison song) ultimately being included on the *At Folsom Prison* LP.

The Folsom shows were more than a strategic move, more than a marketing stunt, more than even just a show of support for a constituency Cash had long supported. These performances were a shot at redemption. "I knew this was it, my chance to make up for all the times when I had messed up," he told Robert Hilburn of the *Los Angeles Times*, who was the lone music journalist covering the event. "I kept hoping my voice wouldn't give out again. Then I suddenly felt calm. I could see the men looking over at me. There was something in their eyes that made me realize everything was going to be okay. I felt I had something they needed."

When *At Folsom Prison* was released in May, Columbia didn't put much effort into supporting or promoting the album. The label was riding high as two albums by Simon & Garfunkel, *Bookends* and the soundtrack to *The Graduate*, were battling it out for Number One on the charts. But the live version of "Folsom Prison Blues" entered the country and pop charts, with one interesting modification from the original tapes. In an unforgettable moment, when Cash sings "I shot a man in Reno/Just to watch him die," the audience of prisoners lets out a wild cheer. This reaction was actually spliced into the recording by Johnston for effect, since the Folsom inmates were under strict orders to stay under control—but it made a haunting, indelible impression.

The song had to go through yet another edit when, eleven days after it charted, Robert F. Kennedy was assassinated. "Folsom Prison" was withdrawn, the "shot a man in Reno" line was removed (over Cash's objections), and then it was sent back out to radio. This didn't slow the single's momentum; it reached Number One on the country charts and hit the pop Top 40.

Johnny Cash and the band inside the Folsom Prison's
cafeteria playing on a makeshift stage, January 13, 1968

The *At Folsom Prison* album continued gaining steam, also hitting Number
One on the country chart and climbing all the way to Number 13 on the pop
side. It remained on the country charts for ninety-two weeks, and in the *Billboard* Top 200 for 124 weeks. The album was certified Gold in the fall of 1968.

Since its release, this record that Columbia had such little faith in has
become universally acknowledged as a classic, one of the landmark albums
in pop music history. *Rolling Stone* ranked it Number 88 in the magazine's
list of the "500 Greatest Albums of All Time," as well as the third-greatest
live album ever, and the Number One "country album every rock fan should
own." CMT named it the third greatest album in country music history,
and the Library of Congress added it to the National Recording Registry.
Fascination with *At Folsom Prison* has never waned, and in 2003, it was
certified Triple Platinum when sales hit three million copies. Additional
tribute was paid later in 2018, when the Mexican norteño band Los Tigres

del Norte followed in Cash's footsteps and became the first major Latin act to play at Folsom since his appearance; they even invited one of the prisoners onstage to play accordion on their rendition of "Folsom Prison Blues." Fifty years to the month after the concert, the album was inducted into the GRAMMY Hall of Fame.

"You can't separate [the *Folsom* record] from the watershed moment it was in his life and in his career," Rosanne Cash told Michael Streissguth in 2008. "That was the hinge [on] which a whole door opened to something else, and also kind of quantified who he was as an artist."

The success was certainly gratifying for Cash, but even before the Folsom album came out, he had other things on his mind. In the few months between the prison concert and the album release, he and June Carter had gotten engaged—and married.

ON FEBRUARY 22, 1968, the Johnny Cash Show was appearing at the London Gardens (later renamed the London Ice House), a hockey arena in London, Ontario, the hometown of Cash's manager Saul Holiff. Johnny and June had just finished singing their latest hit, "Jackson," when he stepped to the microphone and went off script.

"I stopped the show and I said, 'Will you marry me?' on the microphone," he later recounted. "And she said, 'Go on, sing another, sing another, sing another' and I said 'I'm not gonna sing until you answer me—will you marry me?' And she said, 'Sing a song, sing a song.' She turned her back, you know, trying to get somebody in the band to play some music or something. I kept going until she finally said yes. And I said, 'OK, next song.'"

In a deleted scene from Holiff's son Jonathan's documentary, *My Father and the Man in Black*, some audience members said they weren't sure if the proposal was genuine, staged, or part of the usual show. Nevertheless, it became a pivotal part of the Johnny-and-June mythology, and was re-created as a climactic moment in the *Walk the Line* movie.

Later, June would good-naturedly rib Cash about the public proposal. "He asked me to marry him in front of 7,000 people, but I would have liked it if he would have gotten down on his knees and proposed to me," she said on *The Mike Douglas Show* in 1981. "But that wasn't the way it was. It was a great big production."

They were wed just a week later—the day after winning a GRAMMY for "Jackson"—at a church in Franklin, Kentucky. They wanted a small town where a quiet wedding could be held, and the waiting period to get married was shorter in Kentucky than it was in Tennessee.

Cash, thirty-six, wore a black tuxedo with bow tie, while June, thirty-eight, wore a light-colored, knee-length dress with a scalloped hemline. The best man was Merle Kilgore, and Carter's friend Micki Brooks acted as maid of honor. Country Music Hall of Famer George Morgan sang "I Love You Truly" and "Because," and June reportedly cried during both songs.

"Although several locals eased their way into some of the back pews, the balcony section was packed," the *Bowling Green Daily News* later wrote. "It was even reported that local downtown businesses, including Kenneth Cline's grocery store, closed so employees could attend the wedding on this Friday afternoon."

And then it was back to the road. While *At Folsom Prison* continued its triumphant run, Cash didn't release much new music—he put out two more albums in 1968 that were mostly compilations of existing material (*Old Golden Throat* and *Heart of Cash*, which was sold exclusively through television commercials). Aside from the usual tour stops, though, there was another trip of far greater significance.

In the 1960s, Cash had become intrigued by the possibility of visiting Israel, and in 1966 he had made a brief first visit (or, as he termed it, "pilgrimage") to the Holy Land. Two years later, as he was undergoing a religious transformation, June insisted that they take their honeymoon in Israel. She had a dream in which she saw him standing on a mountain in Galilee, preaching to the multitudes with a Bible in his hand. "One might say," Shalom Goldman wrote in *Tablet* magazine, "that in June Carter Cash's view or understanding her new husband could be saved by Jesus only if he were to actually walk in Jesus' footsteps."

Like their good friend Reverend Billy Graham, the Cashes saw Israel's takeover of Jerusalem in the 1967 Six-Day War as having religious significance, helping pave the way for the Messiah's arrival. By the time of their "pilgrimage," East Jerusalem and Bethlehem were thronged with Christian visitors who sought to "walk where Jesus walked." Cash recorded their observations during the trip, as well as the words of their Israeli tour guide, on a portable tape recorder, and built a new album in which these spoken word snippets linked together a set of new gospel songs, most of them written by Cash. "Going to Israel is like going home," he would say. "You see the things you've been singing about all your life."

The Holy Land—Cash's thirtieth album—was released in January 1969. The cover is a photograph of Cash standing in front of the chapel on top of the Mount of the Beatitudes, immediately north of the Sea of Galilee. The unique but oddly compelling record did surprisingly solid business, reaching the country Top 10 and Number 54 on the pop side. One of the tracks was the joyful, old-timey hit single "Daddy Sang Bass," written by Carl Perkins (in a single burst of inspiration, backstage before a show), which spent six weeks at the top of the country chart.

Still, the response to *At Folsom Prison* practically demanded a more commercial follow-up. But when Cash went back behind bars to record another live album in February 1969, he was a very different man than he had been at Folsom thirteen months earlier. In that short time, he had gotten married, kicked his drug habit (or at least made significant strides to do so), reaffirmed his religious conviction, started working with a new agent

"We got married in a fever": Johnny and June at their
wedding reception, Franklin, Kentucky, March 1, 1968

and manager (Marty Klein and Lou Robin), and, of course, experienced his biggest success ever.

This time, the album would be cut at San Quentin, the first place Johnston had called when Cash brought up the idea of a prison album. It would be his fourth performance at the penitentiary, which might help explain the looser, wilder feel on this record. In the documentary of the event, filmed by Granada Television, the voiceover says that "Johnny Cash is a folk singer who can reach out to his audience and become the Western Hero before their eyes."

Throughout the twenty-one-song set (which Cash said "might have been the first" drug-free performance he gave in many years), he can be heard laughing, joking, yelling—the tension of the Folsom concert now takes on a different form, much more of an us-against-them feel, especially when it came to "San Quentin," the song he wrote specifically for this event.

According to the account by the great music journalist Ralph J. Gleason, when Cash sang the line "San Quentin, may you rot and burn in hell," the reaction was palpable. "The cons screamed back," Gleason wrote. "A tall young guard spun around, smacked one fist into the other palm and said 'He's right!' . . . What he did was right on the edge. If he had screwed it up one notch tighter, the joint would have exploded."

OPPOSITE *At San Quentin*, released on Columbia Records in 1969.
TOP Performing at San Quentin State Prison, California, 1969

According to Robert Hilburn, it was decided beforehand that Cash would perform "San Quentin" twice, since it was considered the major new song of the set, though on the record Cash makes it seem as if the encore was a response to audience demand (producer Johnston ultimately chose to include both versions of the song on the album). "During the second rendition," Cash later said, "all I would have had to do was say 'Break!' and they were gone, man."

Cash's attitude during the San Quentin show can be summarized by the famous image of him flipping off a cameraman, a photo that still shows up on T-shirts and posters as one of rock and roll's most iconic expressions of punk spirit. In the liner notes for the 2000 reissue of *At San Quentin*, Cash explained that he was frustrated at having Granada's film crew blocking his view of the audience. When the crew ignored his request to "clear the stage," out came the middle finger.

In addition to the simmering fury of "San Quentin," another song was performed for the first time during this show, a shaggy-dog poem by children's

author and *Playboy* cartoonist Shel Silverstein called "A Boy Named Sue." Cash spontaneously decided to take a shot at "Sue"; neither the TV crew nor his band knew in advance. He read the words off of a lyric sheet onstage, while Perkins fashioned an improvised melody and rhythm and directed the musicians.

The talking blues is the story of a young man's quest for revenge on a father who abandoned him, and whose only input into his life was naming him Sue, which inevitably meant the kid would face ridicule and harassment by everyone he met. Sue grows up tough and mean, and smartens up quickly, but—angered by all the embarrassment and abuse—he swears that he will find and kill his father for giving him "that awful name."

Sue locates his father at a bar and confronts him, saying, "My name is Sue! How do you do? Now you gonna die!" A vicious brawl follows, which sees the two men "kicking and gouging in the mud and the blood and the beer." After the two have beaten each other almost senseless, Sue's father admits that he is indeed the "son of a bitch" that named him Sue but explains that the moniker was given as an act of love. Because he knew that he wouldn't be there for his son, he gave him the name, believing that it would leave him no choice but to "get tough or die." Learning this, Sue and his father reconcile. With his lesson learned, Sue closes the song with a promise to name his son "Bill or George—anything but Sue!"

The San Quentin version of "Sue" became a phenomenon, a hit single like nothing Cash had ever seen. It topped the country and Adult Contemporary charts, and spent three weeks at Number 2 on the pop charts, held off only by the Rolling Stones' "Honky Tonk Women." The song also won a GRAMMY for Best Male Country Vocal Performance.

In *Heartaches by the Number*, journalist Bill Friskics-Warren offers a fascinating comparison between "A Boy Named Sue" and another country novelty song that was a huge hit in 1969, Merle Haggard's "Okie from Musk-ogee." Unlike the condescension in Haggard's song, "Sue" expresses the ways in which "communication, even to the point of conflict, is the best way to breed the tolerance and mutual understanding needed to bridge any Gap." Cash's song was able to cross over to a pop audience, whereas "Okie" connected more exclusively with country listeners; Friskics-Warren attributes this to its more generous attitude—not that the father is necessarily right that he made Sue who he is today, but that "only after mixing it up with him and hearing him out, he finally knows, right or wrong, where the man he now calls 'Pa' is coming from."

With the momentum from "A Boy Named Sue," *At San Quentin* topped the country and pop charts, was nominated for Album of the Year at the GRAMMYs, and eventually matched *At Folsom Prison*'s three-million-plus sales. Cash had whipped off three consecutive Number One country singles; in 1969, between "Daddy Sang Bass" and "A Boy Named Sue," his songs spent eleven weeks in the top spot. He capped off the year by headlining a sold-out Madison Square Garden—the first country artist ever to fill the "World's Most Famous Arena."

Cash performing in 1969 on *The Johnny Cash Show*, which consistently broke new ground for network television by presenting musical giants ranging from Louis Armstrong to Joni Mitchell

JOHNNY CASH WAS NOW A FULL-FLEDGED CELEBRITY. Cameras followed him for a documentary called *The Man, His World, His Music*, in which he joked, "I've learned to adapt very well to prosperity." The film showed him onstage and with the Native American community during his visit to Wounded Knee, but much of it concentrated on a trip back to Dyess, where he is walking through the town center and wandering in the fields, reminiscing about his youth. Cash and sister Louise poke around their now-empty childhood home. They point to the spot where he used to sit in front of the radio, and Louise says, quietly, "At that time, it was a fine house."

Country culture was gaining in stature in 1969. Cash was profiled in *Vogue* and *Time* magazines. Bob Dylan released the unironically countrified *Nashville Skyline* album, featuring liner notes by Cash and opening with a duet by the two singers on "Girl from the North Country." (Cash and Dylan actually recorded a full album's worth of material; though heavily bootlegged, no other songs have been officially released.) Glen Campbell was given a network variety show, and the cornball comedy and music program *Hee Haw* launched. It was perhaps not a shock, then, when ABC approached Cash about a TV show of his own.

The Johnny Cash Show started with an hour-long tryout as a summer replacement for the Saturday night variety extravaganza *The Hollywood Palace*. During the test period, Cash had to compromise by booking old-school showbiz royalty like Bob Hope, Burl Ives, and Peggy Lee, but things would change when he was given the green light in the fall.

The show was recorded at Nashville's Ryman Auditorium, home of Cash's former nemesis the Grand Ole Opry. Cash opened each episode, and all his touring support—June and the Carter Family, Carl Perkins, the comedic stylings of the Statler Brothers—were featured regularly. But the musical guests for the show were daring, even unprecedented. The first episode included Joni Mitchell, Cajun fiddler Doug Kershaw, and a rare appearance by Bob Dylan.

Over the next two years, the range of music presented on *The Johnny Cash Show* was staggering. Stevie Wonder, Creedence Clearwater Revival, Louis Armstrong, James Taylor, Derek and the Dominos, Neil Young, Jerry Lee Lewis—a list of icons and newcomers that was not just dazzling considering the Nashville setting, but coming from any network program then or now.

The show also included a "Country Gold" segment, which featured legends rarely seen on television, such as Bill Monroe and his Blue Grass Boys or the Everly Brothers performing with their father, offering a basic education in the genre's history. Cash returned to his own historical obsessions for a regular segment called "Ride This Train," in which he would perform a medley of thematically linked songs.

Cash stood up to ABC numerous times over their concerns about his content. He refused to cut the word "stoned" from Kris Kristofferson's "Sunday

Morning Coming Down," which he introduced with a monologue invoking his own father: "My Daddy was one of those who hopped a freight train a couple of times to go to look for work. He wasn't a bum. He was a hobo, but he wasn't a bum. I suppose we've all, all of us been at one time or another a drifter at heart, and…. many who have drifted, including myself, have found themselves no closer to peace of mind than a dingy backroom, on some lonely Sunday morning, with it comin' down all around you." He released the performance from the show as a single, and it became a major hit.

He repeatedly brought up his Christian faith despite "network anxieties" about mentioning religion, and he fought to have folk singer Pete Seeger on the show. Seeger's appearance on *The Smothers Brothers Comedy Hour* performing the anti-Vietnam War song "Waist Deep in the Big Muddy" had created a firestorm. Cash premiered the "Man in Black" song, his most explicit social commentary, on a special episode taped at Nashville's Vanderbilt University.

The Johnny Cash Show lasted for fifty-eight episodes, with the final show airing on March 31, 1971. Though it had reached as high as Number 17 in the 1969 Nielsen ratings, viewership started to decline in the fall of 1970 (part of a trend that saw the public tiring of the variety show format), and it was canceled during the "rural purge" of the early '70s in which "everything with a tree in it" was cut from network programming, led by CBS.

In the autobiography, Cash wrote that he was "relieved when ABC didn't renew for a third year," claiming that the show was "demanding, physically and creatively." He went on to say that, in the early '70s, "sometimes it felt like I was just a passenger on the Johnny Cash train, powerless over my destination, speed, or schedule."

Later, Cash would speak even more bitterly of his experience with the series. "I resented all the dehumanizing things that television does to you, the way it has of just sterilizing your head," he told Robert Hilburn. To Larry Linderman from *Penthouse* magazine, Cash said, "I soon came to realize that I was just another piece of merchandise to the network, a cog in their wheel…I felt as if they were stealing my soul."

"He was so extraordinarily famous during those several years [of the TV show] that his life was so hard because of it," Rosanne later said. "If we wanted to go to a movie, he would sometimes rent the theater. If we wanted to go skating, I remember him renting the skating rink. He could not leave his house without being accosted. And I never saw him being anything less than polite and kind to people. I couldn't have done it. I don't know anybody who could."

But his achievement with *The Johnny Cash Show* was immense, providing a platform for both remarkable young artists and overlooked pioneers, and illustrating the common ground that music could provide across races, classes, and generations. Now Cash was unarguably a legend himself, about to return to the studio—and a winding, uneven road.

A THING CALLED LOVE

Johnny and June

"I want a love like Johnny and June," sang Heidi New-field in "Johnny and June," a 2008 hit that would be nominated for Song of the Year by the Academy of Country Music. "Rings of fire burning with you/ Walk the line till the end of time."

The romance between Johnny Cash and June Carter certainly electrified the world—the long-simmering love between a rising star and a (slightly older) member of country music royalty; the epic tale of a woman who rescued a man, not yet her mate, from his addictions and saved his life; their deaths separated by just a few months ("When you're gone/I want to go too," sang Newfield); all played out onstage and on record, night after night. It is, of course, the basis of the Oscar-winning 2005 film, *Walk the Line*, which was not so much a Johnny Cash biopic as a celebration of this celebrated love affair (and is not to be confused with the 1970 crime thriller *I Walk the Line*, starring Gregory Peck and Tuesday Weld, for which Cash wrote the soundtrack).

The story of Johnny and June continues to capture the public imagination. In 2015, the British life insurance company Beagle Street commissioned a poll to select the greatest love letter of all time, in an effort to encourage Brits to be more romantic on Valentine's Day. The winner was a note Cash wrote to Carter in 1994, for her sixty-fifth birthday. "You still fascinate and inspire me," Cash wrote. "You influence me for the better. You're the object of my desire, the #1 Earthly reason for my existence."

A boy named John Carter: a beaming Johnny and June leaving Madison Adventist Hospital, Nashville, with their son, 1970

Cash's missive got more votes than love letters from British Prime Minister Winston Churchill to his wife, poet John Keats (writing to his next-door neighbor), musician Jimi Hendrix (to a mystery woman he calls his "little girl"), and twice-married actors Richard Burton and Elizabeth Taylor. The letter, written twenty-six years into their marriage (and almost forty years after they met), was a reflection on the duration of their love.

"We got old and got used to each other," Cash went on. "We think alike. We read each others minds. We know what the other wants without asking. Sometimes we irritate each other a little bit. Maybe sometimes we take each other for granted. But once in a while, like today, I meditate on it and realize how lucky I am to share my life with the greatest woman I ever met."

In his autobiography, Cash was more understated writing about June. "I'm thankful she's a soul mate," he wrote, "that we can talk to each other sometimes without even speaking, and have an understanding on a lot of things." He almost made it sound easy.

Yet the story of Johnny and June wasn't always simple. "*Walk the Line* is as far as people look sometimes," says John Carter Cash. "And it is true, at the end, they were happier than they ever were—they were happily ever after. But it wasn't a fairy tale after they got married in 1968. There were struggles and inconsisten-

Johnny Cash, literally "born in a cotton patch" (a share-cropper's shack without any windows) February 26, 1932, learned to love folk music at the age of three while listening to the work crews on the "Cotton-Belt" Railroad at his front doorstep.

June Carter, regular member of the Grand Ole Opry and recording star for Liberty Records, has now been touring with the Johnny Cash Show for over a year. Besides mastering the guitar, banjo and autoharp, she is by far the finest comedienne in the business today!

Johnny and June's promotional photos from 1963

cies and addiction, different kinds of darkness, different depths of sadness that came along with chronic abuse of drugs. Their relationship went through struggles and hardship; they were at the edge of divorce at least twice."

The complications started as soon as they laid eyes on each other. When they first met in 1956, backstage at the Grand Ole Opry, June could feel the attraction, but she knew it was dangerous. They were both married, though she would divorce Carl Smith that year.

"I only glanced into his eyes," June later said, describing the moment, "because I believed that I would be drawn into his soul and I would never have been able to walk away . . . he was the most handsome man I'd ever met." She sensed that Cash felt a similar temptation—"both of us afraid to look and both afraid to see the lost and lonely souls that we were."

June was part of the second generation of the Carter Family; the original group of A.P., Sara, and Maybelle Carter was one of country music's true pioneers, recording such standards as "Wabash Cannonball," "Wildwood Flower," and "Can the Circle Be Unbroken." After A.P. and Sara's mar-

riage ended, Maybelle continued to perform with her daughters Anita, June, and Helen.

Cash may have had an ulterior motive in adding the Carters to his touring show in the early 1960s, but it certainly didn't seem suspicious—he was bringing along one of the great dynasties in the genre. Meantime, June had married Edwin "Rip" Nix, a former football player, police officer, and stock car driver, in 1957, and their daughter, Rosey, was born the following year.

For twelve years, Johnny and June circled their wild desire. It came out in the music; there was no denying the lust conveyed in "Ring of Fire" or "Jackson." But Cash was still married to Vivian Liberto, who stayed home raising their four daughters while he spent more and more time on the road, and sank deeper into his drug habit. Liberto lived to see the way Johnny and June's story was told in *Walk the Line* (though the subjects themselves did not), and her memoir was largely written as a response to the Hollywood version of the story.

From the first time Vivian met June, in 1958, she sensed trouble. "This woman was a danger to my family," she wrote. And while

the film portrayed Johnny as the aggressive pursuer and June as the reluctant one, Liberto claimed that it was actually the opposite—most pointedly when she describes an angry backstage confrontation in which June said to her, "Vivian, he will be mine." In her 2010 memoir, *Composed*, Rosanne Cash wrote that her mother "never said an ill word about Dad to us children" but that she cast "a venomous indictment" of June Carter.

It is unclear exactly when the affair between Cash and Carter began, but it clearly tormented the man who had started his career by pledging "I Walk the Line." The cycle of guilt and anger fed his consumption of pills, which in turn left June to try to protect him on tour—ransacking his hotel rooms to find hidden stashes of his drugs and throwing them away ("none of the boys who worked with him would have got rid of his pills," she said, "but I knew if *somebody* didn't do it, we wouldn't get through the tour") and accelerated their dependence on each other.

He was absent as a father, distant even when he was home, and begged Liberto for a divorce that her faith prohibited. (Carter and Nix were divorced in 1966.) When she did consent to the divorce and it was finalized in late 1967, it was barely a few months later before

Backstage before a concert, John and June hug at a party celebrating their first wedding anniversary and John's 37th birthday, Anaheim, March 1, 1969

Handwritten on album: "YOU ARE MY FLOWER"

Handwritten on right side: "TIM, MY DADDY LOVES MY MAMA,"

ABOVE "You're the object of my desire, the #1 Earthly reason for my existence": homemade photo album given to June by Johnny, Christmas 1975. **OPPOSITE** Valentine from Johnny to June, 1992

Cash proposed to June—and the storybook romance that history recognizes really began.

But of course, the marriage itself was never as easy as the public version seemed. As early as 1969, while June was pregnant with their only child together and Johnny's only son, John Carter, she learned that he was or had been having an affair with her sister Anita. In the years before the marriage, Cash and Carter would have fights, break up, and John had affairs with other women, so, Robert Hilburn pointed out, "what happened in 1969 was more like a relapse rather than the starting of a new relationship."

But after John Carter was born, Cash pulled his family tightly around him. It's tough to find a photo from the 1970s in which he's not surrounded by June and the kids. He pulled through his addiction—for the time being— married the woman he loved, and had the son he wanted. The same year John Carter was born, Johnny and June released a version of Tim Hardin's "If I Were a Carpenter"

that became a big hit and won them another GRAMMY for Best Country Vocal Performance by a Duo or Group. The legend of Johnny and June, after the high romantic drama of its beginnings, was now settling into place.

Yet the relationship faced challenges consistently for the next three decades. "They really loved each other, but they struggled," said John Carter Cash. "There were a couple of times when their marriage almost failed. It was partly due to my father's volatility and character and partly due to his addiction issues. That's part of the tale."

In 2007, John Carter wrote *Anchored in Love: An Intimate Portrait of June Carter Cash*, to give an honest and thorough account of his mother and his parents' relationship; it was released in conjunction with a tribute album of the same name, which featured such artists as Elvis Costello, Brad Paisley, Ralph Stanley, and Loretta Lynn (as well as June's daughter Carlene Carter and stepdaughter—a word June

Without a doubt,
The time will come
When flowers fade.
But I'll be there
To comfort you
In evenings' shade.

And you will know
For I will show
In life's last hour
You are my flower
You are my flower
You are my flower

John
Christmas 1975

Feb 15 1992

Dear June,
Valentines is pretty
Valentines is cute.
So is you
So is you.
Happy Valentines day yesterday.
I love you
John

refused to let any of the family use—Rosanne Cash) performing songs associated with June. The book presented the complexities underneath the fairy-tale marriage, in which June lived in denial of relapses in her husband's drug use, maintaining her faith that the good man she loved would always win out. She was compulsive herself, especially when it came to spending money.

Johnny alluded to her wild shopping sprees with good humor in his autobiography. But eventually their homes (in Tennessee, Jamaica, and Virginia) were overloaded with massive pieces of furniture, huge collections of dinner sets, pottery, linens, and silverware. Rather than try to limit the damage or acknowledge the issues underlying the out-of-control spending, Johnny was the perfect enabler.

"My father would come home with pearls, and put 'em around her neck," John Carter said. "He was often the instigator of huge, unnecessary purchases."

In the 1990s, things took a more dangerous turn when the cumulative effect of her family's drug problems combined with the aches of her own aging body to drive June to prescription narcotics. She stopped speaking in full sentences and would drift off into her own world.

"She maintained strong control of her addiction," John Carter said, adding that any attempts at confrontation were pointless. Her husband, needless to say, was reluctant to step in.

And yet Johnny and June persevered— and ultimately, the true story may be more inspiring than the Hollywood version. Having fought so hard to be together, the couple was determined to stay together. And just like in so many Johnny Cash songs, the lesson was that something worth having was worth working for. They stayed on the road—year after year, show after show—together, and then when Johnny's health wouldn't allow him to tour anymore, they seemed to grow even closer, and the mythology around them grew as well.

LEFT The Cash family on vacation in the US Virgin Islands, 1969. RIGHT Johnny, June, and John Carter traveling, ca. 1975

In 2001, Cash included a cover of U2's "One" on the *Solitary Man* album. It's a complicated, often misunderstood song. Not a simple profession of love, Bono's lyric expresses instead the challenges and obligations that come with sharing a life with another person: "We're one, but we're not the same/Well, we hurt each other and we do it again." Cash "added signature gravitas" to the song, wrote *Rolling Stone*, "infusing [the lyrics] with a vitriol Bono could never muster."

Cash spoke to country music journalist Peter Cooper about the recording and his understanding of the song. "A good love affair gone wrong needs some good work on it," he said, going on to talk about the evolution of his relationship with June. "Nobody could ever have a truer companion through the sickness as June was. We're closer now than we've been in our lives."

And to those closest to her, June provided a model for living, for strength. "When I was a young girl at a difficult time," Rosanne Cash once said, "confused and depressed, with no idea of how my life would unfold, she held a picture for me of my adult life: a vision of joy and power and elegance that I could grow into. She did not give birth to me, but she helped me give birth to my future."

"June was one of the great women in this business," says Cash's post-1970 manager Lou Robin. "One minute she would be June Carter Cash and the next minute be Mrs. Johnny Cash, depending on what was coming at her."

Indeed, if there was one real casualty of Johnny and June's marriage, it may have been June Carter Cash's own career as a pioneering woman in country music. In 1975, she released her first solo album, *Appalachian Pride*, but she wouldn't put out another album on her own until 1999's *Press On*, which would win a GRAMMY for Best Traditional Folk Album. Cash expressed concern that June's significance would be overshadowed by her identification as Mrs. Johnny Cash. "I think her contribution to country music will probably go under-recognized simply because she's my wife," he wrote.

But June herself voiced no such sense of disappointment. "I was never looking back in regret," she said. "I never thought, 'Oh, why didn't I become an actress?' or 'Why did I just go paddling along after John?' I've always walked along right by his side, and he's always supported everything I do." Elsewhere, she said simply, "I've always just felt very proud to be walking in the wake of Johnny's fame."

At June's funeral in 2003, Rosanne Cash delivered a eulogy that captured this dedication. "If being a wife were a corporation, June would have been the CEO," she said. "It was her most treasured role. She began every day by saying, 'What can I do for you, John?' Her love filled up every room he was in, lightened

every path he walked, and her devotion created a sacred, exhilarating place for them to live out their married life."

Tom Petty recounted to Sylvie Simmons his observations of June's presence and role at the "American Recordings" sessions he attended. "June to me was the original rock and roll gal—right until the end of her life," he said. "June was there every day, unless she went out shopping or something, and she'd come in with fur boas and all sorts of ornate clothing and talk quite a bit, and you couldn't help but love her. John so depended on June, and he so bounced everything off June. It was just such a deep love that it was great to see how the two of them were such a team, really involved in everything together, including the music."

A week after June died, Johnny insisted on going back to work, getting in the studio and recording as much music as he could.

"Some people said 'You're crazy, you shouldn't do this that soon,'" he said. "And I said, 'Tell me why I shouldn't . . . I have to.'"

"June told me once, 'If something happens to me that I can't work, you keep working. You have to work.' She knows me, that I have to work."

He made it four months without her. He recorded dozens more songs. And then he, too, was gone. And if it happened that way for someone else, we would say that they were just like Johnny and June.

Johnny and June performing together, ca. 1974

ONE PIECE AT A TIME

6

THIS PAGE Some of the world's greatest songwriters joined Cash at his lakefront home in Hendersonville for his famous "guitar pulls," including this one, ca. 1974.

PREVIOUS Cash performs at a Billy Graham rally in Central Park, New York City, September 22, 1991.

1975–1993

ohnny Cash succinctly summed up the first four decades of his career in his autobiography. "My star came on strong in the mid-'50s," he wrote, "cooled in the early and mid-'60s, reignited with a vengeance in '68, burned brightly until '71 and then dimmed again." Coming off of the triumphant run that carried him from *At Folsom Prison* through *The Johnny Cash Show* and made him an international icon, his work rapidly entered a very different phase.

Personally, all seemed right for Cash, with his wife and his young son by his side; he seemed committed to making up for time spent away from his wife and daughters in the previous decade. Creatively, he continued to feel energized. But commercially, the wheels started to fall off. "The 1970s for me were a time of abundance and growth," he wrote. "[They] also saw the implosion of my recording career."

The contrast was sudden and dramatic. Through 1973, Cash's albums were peaking in the Top 5 on the country charts, most reaching the top spot. Starting in 1974, his releases all stalled in the high 20s or low 30s—if they made the charts at all. Between 1973 and 1979, he would have one Top 10 single.

Changes were taking place all around—beginning with the sound and community in Nashville, in large part because of the rock acts Cash was bringing into town for his television show. In the late 1960s and early 1970s, dozens of rock and folk acts traveled to Tennessee and, in a series of unlikely alliances, emerged with an impressive number of big hits and classic recordings. (The era was documented in 2015 with an exhibition at the Country

Johnny Cash is kissed by his wife, June Carter, after he was inducted into the Country Music Hall of Fame at the Country Music Association's awards presentations night, October 13, 1980. Looking on is their son, John.

Music Hall of Fame titled *Dylan, Cash and the Nashville Cats: A New Music City.*) Between the Cash show, Bob Dylan's use of the city as his recording base for several years, and an extraordinary group of session musicians informally known as the Nashville Cats, there was a great migration to the studios on Music Row that produced albums by Neil Young, Leonard Cohen, Linda Ronstadt, Simon & Garfunkel, and three of the four Beatles, among others.

Concurrently, the late '60s and early 1970s saw a transformation in the sound and structure of mainstream country music. Cash's success notwithstanding, the previous decade had largely seen them growing smoother and more sophisticated—a sound being called "countrypolitan." Producers Billy Sherrill and Glenn Sutton were adding string arrangements and choral background vocals to records by Tammy Wynette, Glen Campbell,

ABOVE AND OPPOSITE Cash on location on Mount Arbel in Galilee, Israel, filming *The Gospel Road*, the story of the life of Jesus, 1971. The project was the fulfillment of a lifelong dream for Cash.

Lynn Anderson, and Charlie Rich, and scoring major hits that sometimes crossed over to a pop market.

More pop stars began embracing the countrypolitan approach and creating more of a country-pop hybrid. Olivia Newton-John was named the Female Vocalist of the Year at the 1974 CMA awards, and, in an unforgettable incident the next year, Charlie Rich announced that John Denver won the Entertainer of the Year prize over Waylon Jennings, Loretta Lynn, Ronnie Milsap, and Conway Twitty—and then Rich set fire to the card with Denver's name printed on it.

A backlash was setting in, however. Jennings and Willie Nelson were pushing back against the conservative attitudes of their label, RCA. In 1972, Nelson left the company for Atlantic Records (where he had a fan in the legendary producer/executive Jerry Wexler) and recorded a pair of critically acclaimed records, *Shotgun Willie* and the concept album *Phases and Stages*. RCA didn't want to lose Jennings as well, so they granted him the autonomy to produce his own records. Jennings responded with the groundbreaking *Honky Tonk Heroes* and *This Time* albums.

Nelson's *Red Headed Stranger* album exploded even bigger in 1975, and the two artists were now being credited with spearheading a new subgenre called "outlaw country," characterized by its rock rhythms, erudite lyrics,

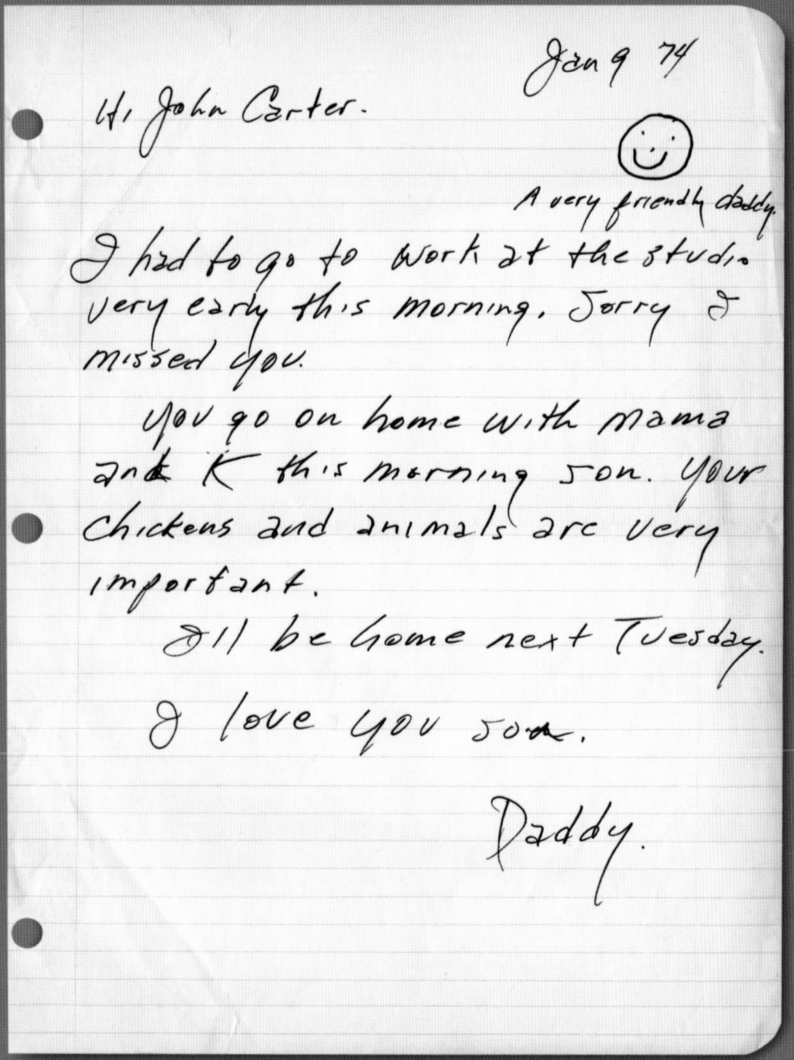

Jan 9 74

Hi, John Carter.

A very friendly daddy

I had to go to work at the studio very early this morning. Sorry I missed you.

You go on home with mama and K this morning son. Your chickens and animals are very important.

I'll be home next Tuesday.

I love you son.

Daddy.

ABOVE "A very friendly daddy": a note Johnny wrote to his son, John Carter, after returning from Jamaica, January 9, 1974. OPPOSITE Johnny with John Carter at the circus

Johnny and June with President Gerald Ford in the Oval Office, 1975. Cash's other meetings with presidents included performing for Richard Nixon and receiving the National Medal of Arts from George W. Bush.

and independent spirit.In 1976, a compilation of previously released material by Nelson, Jennings, Jessi Colter, and Tompall Glaser titled *Wanted! The Outlaws* became the first country album to be certified Platinum for selling a million copies.

Cash didn't sit comfortably on either side of this artistic divide. Though Jennings was an old friend and Cash would later join forces with Waylon and Willie for the Highwaymen supergroup, at the time he was much too identified with family and faith to fully embrace the "outlaw" designation. Instead, he took on the most ambitious religion-oriented project of his life, the film and double album soundtrack *The Gospel Road*.

The movie was the fulfillment of June's 1968 dream of Johnny standing on a mountain in Israel, holding a Bible in his hand, and was inspired by the couple's friendship with Billy Graham. Cash took the documentary-style storyline from Thompson's Concordance, a biblical reference book, and cowrote the script with guitarist Larry Murray. The self-financed film was shot during a return to Israel in 1971 with a cast, crew, and entourage of about thirty people, including Robert Elfstrom, who both directed and appeared on screen as a (nonspeaking) Jesus Christ.

The album consists primarily of spoken segments taken from the film, interspersed with songs. In addition to Johnny and June, tour regulars the Carter Family and the Statler Brothers contributed vocals, as did Kris Kristofferson and Rita Coolidge. Released in 1973, the soundtrack could be considered a success in reaching Number 12 on the country charts; the single, "Children," made it to Number 30—a long way from Cash's recent heights, but certainly acceptable for a gospel record .

Yet Cash's attitude toward his secular music prospects was turning sour. In 1974, he wrote in the autobiography, "I underwent a kind of mental divorce from the CBS power structure on Music Row . . . it was hard to get excited about an album project when I knew the people at my label had come to regard me as a long shot." For the rest of the decade, he didn't expect much in the way of label support or commercial viability. "I went through the mid-'70s doing my own thing," he wrote, "making my own albums my own way."

In an interview, though, he expressed a bit more doubt in some of his own creative choices. "Everything that I have released, I was proud of it at that time," he told Patrick Carr of *Country Music* magazine in 1974, "but the public has a way of proving you wrong."

John Carter Cash indicates that his father's priorities were evolving. "What was most important to my father changed after *Gospel Road*," he says. "After that, family home life became most important to Dad. Creatively, he started looking around and going in different directions, but he cared most about the boy at home and his wife. And traveling on the road and playing his music."

Albums like *The Junkie and The Juicehead Minus Me* or *John R. Cash* (a record he particularly disliked; he cut his vocals separately from the backing tracks, which were recorded by a group of hot-shot session musicians) sputtered on the charts and the radio, but touring was always reliable, so the Johnny Cash Show never slowed down. "I love the road," he wrote. "I love being a gypsy. In some important ways I live for it, and in other ways it keeps me alive . . . it's adventure, companionship, creativity, freedom."

In fact, since joining the team in 1970, manager Lou Robin had been developing a touring strategy that proved crucial to Cash's career, looking beyond the United States and making him a truly international artist. "It was incumbent on me to find new horizons," says Robin. "I tried to open up new markets for John, which was very easy to do since his music was known worldwide." They started with England, expanding to the European continent, Australia, and New Zealand.

"It meant he didn't have to go back and play Green Bay every year. We had enough places in the world to go with him—Eastern Europe, two weeks to go across Canada, forty-four thousand over two nights in Prague. There was a lot of trail-blazing, but he was always amenable to going and conquering new horizons." The Bellamy Brothers ("Let Your Love Flow") toured with Cash in Europe, and learned quickly that his popularity transcended language. "If you were ever at a loss for translation for anything," says David Bellamy, "you could just say 'Johnny Cash,' because they all understood that."

In the mid-'70s, Cash also started to turn more of his attention away from music. He tried acting, and over the next dozen years appeared in numerous television dramas (*Columbo*, *Little House on the Prairie*, *Dr. Quinn Medicine Woman*) and various made-for-TV movies. He also filmed commercials for Amoco and STP (not the most popular corporations during the days of the energy crisis and gas shortages), and for Lionel Trains, for which he also wrote the music. As for the revenues from the ads, he said, "I use the money I make to do a little good now and then."

Some of these projects seemed more personal than others. In 1974, he hosted *Ridin' the Rails: The Great American Train Story* on ABC, giving him a chance to explore a lifelong obsession yet again. The hour-long special saw Cash walking through different moments in railroad history (Peter Cooper racing a steam locomotive against a horse in 1830, the golden spike linking the eastern and western rail systems in 1869), recounting the action and offering relevant songs—"The Night They Drove Old Dixie Down," "The Legend of John Henry's Hammer," "City of New Orleans." At the conclusion of the show, he seemed to be speaking about more than just trains when he somberly intoned, "Americans ignore the cry of the disappearing railroad.... All the coaches still run, but somehow, they're just not quite the same anymore."

As a result of all these media activities, Cash in some ways remained as familiar a name as he had been at his peak a few years earlier, especially when he scored another fluke hit in 1976. "One Piece at a Time" was a hilarious story of a Detroit autoworker who assembles a car out of parts he swipes from the plant over many years. Not as deep as its story-song predecessor, "A Boy Named Sue," the song still struck a chord (maybe similar to the sentiment of Johnny Paycheck's "Take This Job and Shove It," which would become a huge hit soon after) and shot to Number One on the country charts. The *One Piece at a Time* album was notable for a few other reasons—it was the first release in years credited to "Johnny Cash and the Tennessee Three," and it included the song "Love Has Lost Again," written by Rosanne Cash, who would soon be launching her own recording career.

Cash was seen as such a universally beloved figure that in 1976, he was chosen as the Grand Marshal of the United States Bicentennial Parade. It was validation of words spoken a few years earlier by Richard Nixon, who said that Cash "belongs to the whole country ... a singer not just of country music but of American music that speaks to all Americans."

But this uptick in popularity would prove temporary. The momentum from *One Piece at a Time* fizzled, and the next few albums stumbled again. What's more, Cash admitted that he continued to struggle in his fight against his drug addictions. "Even after I quit in '67, I goofed up a few times," he said

Cash serving as grand marshal of the United States
Bicentennial Parade, Washington, DC, 1976; his father,
Ray, is driving. A few years earlier, President Richard
Nixon had said that Cash "belongs to the whole country."

in 1976. "There were three or four times when I had to keep relearning my
lesson that I can't mess with it or I'm dead."

Columbia Records had lost any sense of what to do with Johnny Cash. It's
not that the late-1970s albums are bad; they're just unfocused and ultimately
undistinguished. In 1979, Columbia took their most aggressive approach with
the *Silver* album, attempting to update Cash's sound with producer Brian
Ahern, known for his work with Emmylou Harris. They added digital filters
and phase shifters along with extra musicians and horn players. Cash did
have one hit from this effort at modernization—ironically, a version of the
traditional cowboy song "(Ghost) Riders in the Sky," which reached Number
2 on the country charts.

In interviews from the time, mostly it sounds as if Cash, frustrated and
adrift, has checked out of his own recording career. "I want more time for

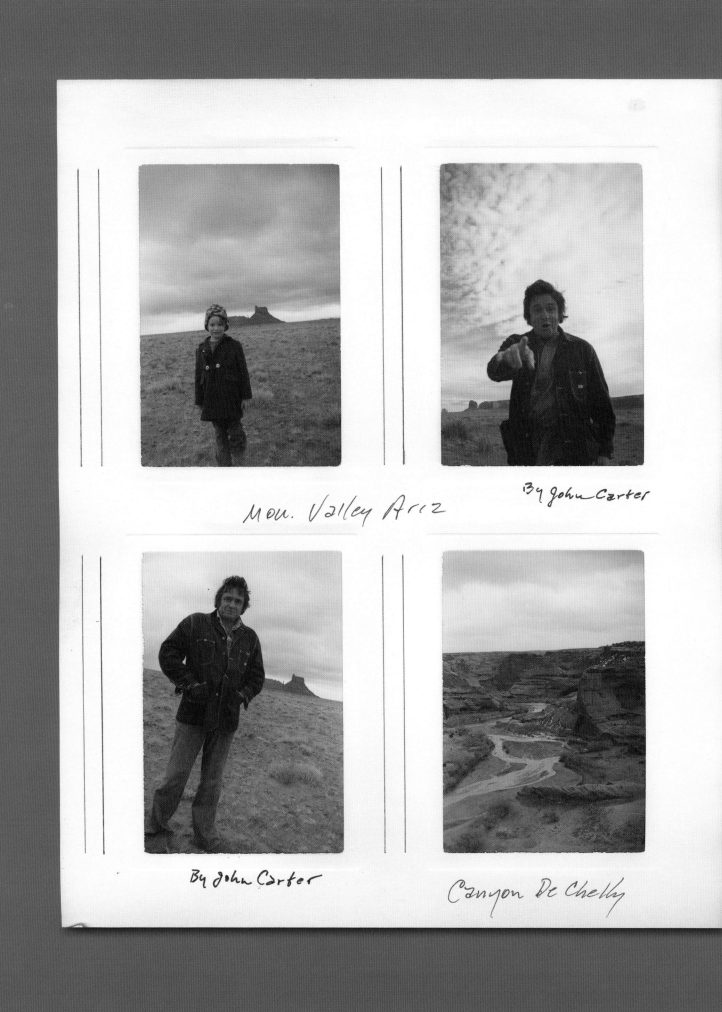

Mou. Valley Ariz

By John Carter

By John Carter

Canyon De Chelly

OPPOSITE AND ABOVE John Carter's and June's family snapshots in Monument Valley, Arizona, ca. 1975. In his Sun Records days, Cash had wanted to record the songs of the Old West, and he eventually released *Sings the Ballads of the True West* in 1965.

In and around Cinnamon Hill, the Cash home in Jamaica, ca. 1977. Cash compared the rural beauty of the area to his boyhood home in Arkansas.

LEFT Poster for the final Highwaymen tour in Australia and New Zealand, 1995. The Highwaymen (Cash, Kris Kristofferson, Waylon Jennings, and Willie Nelson) formed in 1985; Marty Stuart, Cash's former son-in-law and a GRAMMY-winning recording artist and music historian, once recalled that when the supergroup began to play together, "the magic was tangible—you could feel it in the air." **RIGHT** Cash's handwritten song selection for future Highwaymen recordings, 1995

myself," he told Patrick Carr in 1979, "and I want more freedom from worry and work and the hassle that goes on at the offices and the recording studios."

In 1980, as the pop-flavored "Urban Cowboy" boom was setting the tone in Nashville, Cash was inducted into the Country Music Hall of Fame, a remarkable distinction—at age forty-eight, he was the youngest living person to have been so honored. "Songwriter, historian, fighter of causes; friend to the deprived and troubled, friend of great men, a leader in the temporal world, and follower in the spiritual world, Johnny Cash is the total entertainer," read the text on his Hall of Fame plaque. "The Man in Black retains his roots in the soil as he grows in conscience and integrity."

It would be the last good news Cash would have for a while.

IN 1981, CASH TEAMED UP WITH countrypolitan producer Billy Sherrill for *The Baron*, a decent-selling album whose title track was a rare return to country's Top 10. But before the record could provide a new push to Cash's career, he was injured in an incident that would have been comic if it hadn't had such serious consequences.

In addition to the offices, museum, studio, and gift shop at Hendersonville's "House of Cash" complex, there was also an enclosed area with exotic animals. It was here that, Cash noted in a particularly deadpan tone in the autobiography, "I was almost killed by an ostrich."

It was an especially cold winter, and the female ostrich of the pair Cash kept had frozen to death—an event, he hypothesized, which might have been the reason for her mate's aggression. Cash was walking through his property when the ostrich jumped out, spread his wings, and hissed at him. Knowing he would have to pass by the bird on his way back, Cash picked up a big stick, and when the ostrich started to come at him, he took a swing—and missed. The bird flew up and then landed on Cash, breaking two ribs and ripping open his stomach. Cash landed on a rock, breaking three more ribs, and finally chased off the ostrich with the piece of wood.

The hospital stitched up the wounds, but Cash was hurting, and there lay the trouble. "That's what painkillers are for," he wrote, "so I felt perfectly justified in taking lots of them. Justification ceased to be relevant after that; once the pain subsided completely I knew I was taking them because I liked the way they made me feel. And while that troubled my conscience, it didn't trouble it enough to keep me from going down that old addictive road again."

When the pills upset his stomach, he started drinking wine. The alcohol also helped take the edge off of the amphetamines he was taking "because I was still looking for that euphoria."

"When that ostrich broke his ribs and he got addicted to pain pills, who he was changed," says John Carter Cash. "The man that I knew earlier went away. There were a lot of arguments in the house. They fired the entire band, then hired a few people back."

Cash rallied enough to host *Saturday Night Live* in April 1982, with musical guest Elton John. But tensions between Johnny and June were rising, coming to a boil during a tour stop in Montreux, Switzerland. According to John Carter Cash, June had decided to leave Johnny following the show, which marked the end of a European tour. She told her husband to go back home, and said that she would stay in Switzerland with their son—which she did, for a week. "We stayed and ate caviar and blinis," says John Carter, "but after that she went back and forgave him."

He recounts another incident when he felt that their marriage was on its last legs. "I was in Jamaica with [my parents] and they were screaming at each other in the house, and my dad turned to me and said, 'Son, go to your room.' And I thought for sure they were going to call me in and tell me they were getting divorced. I came back in and my mother had this glowing look in her eye and she said, 'We're getting married again!' And they re-established their vows, and there was a great healing at that time."

But Cash's run of bad luck continued when a group of armed, masked robbers invaded his home in Jamaica on Christmas Day of 1982. As he recounts the story, he and his family were able to talk calmly to the invaders and defuse the danger of the situation, to a point where the inexperience and incompetence of the attackers almost seemed laughable, but the episode was certainly still traumatic.

His use of amphetamines continued to increase until a 1983 incident in which he trashed a hotel room in Nottingham, UK, and ended up in the hospital. His family organized an intervention, and afterward Cash agreed to check into the Betty Ford Center in Rancho Mirage, California. In the wire service news story that ran at the time, Cash's sister Reba was quoted saying that he "wants to make sure he doesn't have a problem" because "he had a drug problem in the past, twenty years ago." She added that Cash had suffered severe back spasms and also underwent "extensive" surgery for an ulcer that was aggravated during his recent European tour. She said he also had surgery on his hand, and "he wants to suffer no ill effects from the painkillers he had to take."

In the clinic, Cash befriended fellow patient Ozzy Osbourne, and also worked on some of the songs that would not see light of day until the *Out Among the Stars* album was eventually released in 2014. The lessons and exercises of his treatment presumably inspired lyrics like those in "Came to Believe," in which he sings about surrendering, asking for help, and developing a spiritual belief in a "power much higher" than himself.

He made records through all of this chaos, among them the impressively tough-edged *Johnny 99* in 1983, which included two gutsy Bruce Springsteen covers and closed with a version of George Jones's "I'm Ragged but I'm Right." Still, there was no place for Johnny Cash on the charts or the airwaves.

In 1984, Cash's music seemed to hit bottom. He put out a self-parodying recording titled "Chicken in Black," about having his brain transplanted into a chicken and receiving a bank robber's brain in return. "The last record I gave CBS was called 'Chicken in Black' and it was intentionally atrocious," he wrote.

But Robert Hilburn disputes the idea that Cash chose to record a deliberately poor song in protest against Columbia's treatment of him. He points out that Columbia presented Cash with the song, and Cash—viewing it as another novelty song along the lines of his big hits "A Boy Named Sue" and "One Piece at a Time"—accepted enthusiastically, performing the song onstage and filming a music video in which he dressed up in a super hero-like bank robber costume. His feelings about the song changed when Jennings told Cash that he looked "like a buffoon" in the video, which aired on Cash's 1984 Christmas TV special. After that, Cash demanded that Columbia withdraw the video from broadcast and recall the single from stores, and he termed the venture "a fiasco."

With Waylon Jennings, 1974. Jennings later wrote
that if the one-time roommates had continued
their earlier drug and alcohol habits, "we probably
would've bottomed out and killed ourselves."

That same Christmas, however, he scored a new triumph when he
returned to Montreux, for a performance with Kris Kristofferson, Waylon
Jennings, and Willie Nelson. "It seemed like a family vacation, just a big
get-together," Marty Stuart (who played in Cash's band at the time) later
recalled. Beyond the actual concert, he spoke of the "guitar pull" at the hotel,
at which the four icons sat around playing for fun. "The magic in that hotel
room, it was tangible—you could feel it in the air, you could almost put it
in your pocket."

John Carter Cash, then a teenager, spoke of the "essential spirit of eager
excitement" during the trip. "The idea just came up to do a record together,"
he said, "out of the joyous camaraderie that everyone was sharing."

Soon the quartet gathered in the studio with producer Chips Moman.
Their version of the Jimmy Webb song "Highwayman" came out first and
became a Number One country hit. That song gave the title to the ten-song
album, which also reached the top spot on the charts. The material ranged
from songs by Woody Guthrie and Bob Seger to Cash's own "Big River." This

Mount Rushmore of country music wasn't actually called The Highwaymen at first—the album was credited to "Nelson, Jennings, Cash, Kristofferson." By the time they took on a band name, the project had only served to help secure their legends and their legacies.

Cash spoke fondly of the collaboration, though he noted feeling that "I don't know Willie very well…he's a hard man to know." The group would go on to release two more studio albums, with a live album and DVD to follow in 2016.

In 1986, Cash joined forces with another group of immortal peers. He returned to Sun Studio in Memphis to team up with Roy Orbison, Jerry Lee Lewis, and Carl Perkins for the album *Class of '55*, produced by Chips Moman for release on his America/Smash label. Only after the sessions did Moman obtain permission from Columbia to use Cash; he put up $100,000 for the right to keep him on the record. The album was a moderate success (though *Village Voice* critic Robert Christgau called it "pathetic"); it spun off a television special and a companion album, *Interviews from the Class of '55 Recording Sessions*, and won a GRAMMY for Best Spoken Word Album.

Changes continued in rapid succession. In 1986, Cash published his one and only novel, *Man in White*, the story of the biblical figure Saul and his conversion to become the Apostle Paul. "Dad went into a renaissance after he got out of Betty Ford," says John Carter Cash. "He came out of his shell and wrote *Man in White*. He was in a good space by then, he was bright, and that's when his scholarly side really came out. He focused and studied. I think it was secondary at that time for him to be worried about music—he was creative, but he didn't have to be the next big country star. It wasn't about that to him, it was that maybe there was a point of redefinition that was coming."

Unsure what to do with an artist with whom they had been affiliated for more than twenty-five years, Columbia Records dropped Johnny Cash, and he signed with the Mercury label. The new company paired him once again with his old friend "Cowboy" Jack Clement for *Johnny Cash Is Coming to Town*. Whatever his frustrations with this phase of his career, his friendship with his old Sun colleague remained a bright spot. They worked on four albums between 1986 and 1991, and Cash later said that "the happiest period of my recording career was when I was working here [in Nashville] with Jack Clement in the '80s."

The touring groundwork that Lou Robin had helped lay down was now serving Cash well; even if his recording career was in limbo, he had no trouble filling the quota of 100 shows per year that he had set for himself. "Some artists go dry for a while," says Robin, "but there were always so many options for him, we never went hungry. We could go anywhere as long as he didn't go back year after year, which was what a lot of country artists were stuck with. That's why we wanted to make him known all over the world."

At a 1987 show filmed for the PBS series *Austin City Limits*, Cash introduced "Sunday Morning Coming Down" with some words of reflection. "That's important for me to do, to look back on where I've been, because I don't want to lose track of where I am trying to go," he said. "I don't even remember the bad times, there have been so many good times."

IN 1988, AT AGE FIFTY-SIX, Cash went to the hospital to visit Waylon Jennings, who was recovering from a heart attack. Jennings suggested that Cash, who had already been diagnosed with diabetes, have his own heart condition checked out. The doctors found that the arteries leading to his heart were blocked, and Cash underwent double bypass surgery, later saying that he had what he called a "near death experience" during the operation. There were further complications when he contracted double pneumonia after the surgery.

One small but surprising sign of encouragement was 1988's *Til Things Are Brighter* album, a tribute to Cash assembled by Jon Langford of the punk pioneers the Mekons and Marc Riley, former member of the Fall and later a BBC DJ. The album included such unexpected Cash fans as Michelle Shocked, Pete Shelley of the Buzzcocks, and Mary Mary, the (male) singer of Gaye Bikers on Acid (concerns that Cash might not be enthusiastic about being covered by someone in a band of that name proved unfounded; he found it amusing).

Cash also reasserted his commitment to social issues and his open-mindedness by endorsing the donation of the album's proceeds to AIDS research—at the time, AIDS was still regarded as an exclusively gay issue, and many prominent people were wary of any association with the disease. "I'm very honored that they did it," Cash told the BBC. "The younger people have picked up the records and picked out these songs and analyzed them, and they know what they're all about—the songs of protest, like the American Indian ballads and a lot of the songs that express a social conscience, a social concern."

His health kept him out of the studio for a while, but Cash returned in 1990 with his own *Boom Chicka Boom* album and the *Highwaymen 2* reunion summit. The solo record felt a bit more personal and good-humored. On "Harley," about a hapless factory worker who gets rich quick, he sang that the title character's wife gives "all of Harley's hard-earned money to the Lord/Harley started drinking, wound up in Betty Ford." The more modest songs worked the best; the biggest disappointment was an inappropriately stylized, self-consciously enigmatic take on Elvis Costello's "Hidden Shame."

The material on *Highwaymen 2* was predictably generic and self-mythologizing, focusing on road songs, trains, and manly self-reliance. "Songs That Make a Difference," which Cash wrote, invoked Bob Dylan, Joni Mitchell, and Roy Orbison in a wistful look back at the days when rock was discovering Nashville just as these stars were turning tail and fleeing.

In 1990, Cash began a physical battle that would last the rest of his days when he endured a botched oral surgery. "The next five years," wrote Nicholas Dawidoff, "were a farrago of infection, surgery, and nerve damage." Touring would begin to be curtailed, and the relationship with Mercury was not panning out.

Cash, front left, and Rolling Stones guitarist Keith
Richards, second from right, jam with Sid McGinnis (rear
left), Steve Cropper (over Cash's shoulder), U2 guitarist
The Edge (rear center), and Little Richard (far right), at his
induction into the Rock and Roll Hall of Fame, New York,
January 16, 1992

"I was very happy for a little while" at the label, Cash wrote, but
said that he had reached a breaking point by 1991, when, he asserted
hyperbolically, "they only pressed 500 copies of my last Mercury album,
The Mystery of Life." The record itself was scraped together out of a few
new sessions and leftovers from the *Johnny Cash Is Coming to Town*
album, padded with new versions of "Hey Porter" and "Wanted Man,"
his one disappointing writing collaboration with Bob Dylan. Still,
wrote country music journalist and historian Alanna Nash, Cash's
"stature is such that he can put out an album like this one and make it work,
after a fashion."

For the first time since signing with Sun in 1955, Johnny Cash didn't
have a record contract. He was resigning himself to a future in Branson,
Missouri, the odd mecca for aging country singers where folks like Andy
Williams, Glen Campbell, and Tony Orlando headlined permanent resi-
dencies at their own theaters; and where Dolly Parton's Dixie Stampede

sat alongside amusement parks, go-kart tracks, and miniature golf courses.

"I'd given up," Cash later wrote. "I'd already started thinking that I didn't want to deal with record companies anymore. Saying goodbye to that game and just working the road, playing with my friends and family for people who really wanted to hear us, seemed very much like the thing to do. I began looking forward to it." But there were also indications that maybe things weren't as bad as they seemed.

In 1992, Cash was inducted into the Rock and Roll Hall of Fame, in a class that also included a host of soul music immortals—the Isley Brothers, Sam and Dave, Bobby "Blue" Bland, and Booker T & the MGs. During the jam session that ended the evening, Cash sang "Big River" backed by a band with Keith Richards, Carlos Santana, and John Fogerty.

Also contributing to that performance was U2 guitarist The Edge, and it would be U2—probably the biggest band in the world at the time—that would provide the next sign of Cash's resurgence. Bono had written a song, inspired by the book of Ecclesiastes, that he said he could only hear Johnny Cash singing. Working titles included "The Preacher," "Wandering," and "Johnny Cash on the Moon." The lyrics describe a man searching for God in a posta-pocalyptic world: "I went out walking, with a bible and a gun/The word of God lay heavy on my heart."

In one interview, Bono explained that though he had many "father figures" in his life, Johnny Cash was somewhere near the top of the list. "I think he was a very godly man, but you had the sense that he had spent his time in the desert." The minimal, atmospheric pulse of the song—which was eventually titled "The Wanderer" and became the final track on U2's 1993 *Zooropa* album—ends with Cash singing "I left with nothing, nothing but the thought of you. I went wandering." U2 producer Flood, who engineered the album, said that he was trying to create the sound of a "completely cold, dis-passionate-sounding Johnny Cash. Almost like he's Johnny Cash the robot."

The recording with U2 demonstrated that Johnny Cash was down but not out. He was approached by the organizers of Lollapalooza, the travel-ing alternative-music festival, but Rosanne warned against it, concerned that it might turn him into an undignified mascot. The backer of Branson's "Cash Country Theater" ran out of money and the building never opened—presumably a disappointment at the time, but ultimately a bullet dodged. ("He had already determined that he wasn't going to stay in Branson the rest of his life, he wanted to go back on the road," says John Carter Cash.) And some of the things Cash was saying proved to be prophetic. "My new stuff is going to be real sparse," he said to music writer Steve Pond in 1992. "I'm gonna keep it real clean and bare."

He described a dream project, an acoustic record that he was calling *Johnny Cash: Late and Alone*. "I'd like to do really hard songs and gut songs and say things that you don't hear these days.... I want to make some records that people will pay attention to."

WHAT IS TRUTH

—

Religion

From the time he walked into the Sun Records offices and told Sam Phillips that he wanted to be a gospel singer and, for one of his last recordings, revisit the hymns of his childhood, there would be no way to separate Johnny Cash's faith from his music. The man who once described himself as a "C-Minus Christian" recorded more than a dozen gospel albums and another four Christmas records—at both high and low moments in his career, with seemingly no concern for the possible effect on his sales momentum—produced and financed a film about the life of Jesus, and even recorded an audiobook in which he read the entire New Testament.

Beyond the projects specifically devoted to his religion and the explicitly sacred material in his repertoire, though, Cash's sense of religious belief, principles, and responsibilities ran through all of his work and all of his life. "My mother never minded me singing rock and roll and country music," he said, "because every time I recorded an album there was always a gospel song included to make her happy." It was his message of tolerance and love that defined Cash's spiritual impact.

"Johnny Cash doesn't sing to the damned," Bono once wrote, "he sings with the damned, and sometimes you feel he might prefer their company."

....

OPPOSITE TOP With Billy Graham at Graham's home in North Carolina, Christmas, 1977. OPPOSITE BOTTOM Performing with June and others at Explo 72, which was dubbed the "Christian Woodstock," in Dallas, June 1972. Graham said of his friendship with Cash, "We were just brothers in Christ."

This commitment to his faith wasn't what everyone wanted to hear from Johnny Cash, and it made for an especially easy target during the commercial lulls in his career. "My record company would rather I be in prison than in church," he once said. In 1974, even his friend Waylon Jennings said that Cash had "sold out to religion." In his 1977 book *Country: The Twisted Roots of Rock 'n' Roll*, Nick Tosches was even harsher. "I have a very low opinion of Johnny Cash," he wrote. "[He] is one of these guys who makes terrible music and just calls on God for an excuse. I think someday, God's going to kick him in the ass."

But Cash accepted the blows he sometimes had to take. In the autobiography, he wrote about one of the things his Christian beliefs meant to him: "You have to be willing to give up worldly things in order to stay true to your faith." It was the honesty in his principles, the willingness to admit his mistakes and his sins

BILLY GRAHAM
Montreat, N.C. 28757
April 19, 1975

My dear John,

Thank you for yours of April 13. I was so
thrilled by the content of your note that tears
came to my eyes. Beloved friend, how I love
you in the Lord. There is no doubt that you
are growing in the grace and knowledge of our
Lord Jesus Christ -- and God has a mighty
ministry for you in the years ahead. The
thing that thrills me is the humble and child-
like faith that you have in our Lord. This is
what thrills the heart of God.

I hope you all have a wonderful time at
Cinnamon Hill. I wish we could be with you.
I have just finished ten thrilling days in
Washington where I had some of the greatest
opportunities of witness that I have ever had
-- from the President on down. I even went
over and testified as to the character of
John Connally. That was only my second time
in Court -- and I hope my last!

With warmest affection to June, John Carter and
the others,

Billy

Mr. Johnny Cash
Cinnamon Hill
St. John's Parish
Little River Post Office
JAMAICA

cc. Tennessee

LEFT Letter from Billy Graham to Cash in Jamaica, 1975. **RIGHT** L. R. Rosey Nix (Johnny's stepdaughter), John Carter Cash, Johnny, and Rosanne Cash, Czechoslovakia, 1978

and not to judge others, that enabled him to reach both conservative churchgoers and renegade rockers. "I wondered how it was possible for a man to maintain constituencies in the widely separated countries of Bob Dylan and Billy Graham," wrote Dorothy Gallagher in *Redbook* in 1971—but really, everyone could sense Cash's conviction and integrity.

Old-time religion ran deep in his veins. His father's father, William Henry Cash, was a "circuit rider"—a traveling preacher—in Arkansas. Carrie Cash, in church and at home, surrounded her family with music steeped in giving glory to God. Remarkably, the death of his beloved,

pious brother Jack, rather than shaking his faith, served to reinforce his devotion.

He believed God was not a wrathful or vindictive force but an accessible and welcoming power. "God is a God to sing to or to sing about," he wrote in the liner notes to the *Love God Murder* box set. "To me, God likes a Southern accent and He tolerates country music and quite a bit of guitar." In his interviews with Sylvie Simmons for the *Unearthed* compilation he said, "God to me has always been a friend that I can call on, that was always there, ready to listen, and it was always my fault if I didn't call on him enough."

The foundation of his faith only seemed to grow stronger for Cash as his life went on. In 1975, he said that during his rise to the top, "I used to sing all those gospel songs, but I never really felt them." But, he went on to say, "I'm not playing [at] church now. I was brought up in the church when I was a boy, and I didn't play [at] church then."

Not that the spiritual and moral center of his songwriting was sappy or simplistic. Jon Pareles of the *New York Times* perceptively noted that the characters in Cash's songs often "face unforgiving elements and indifferent fate; their faith and virtue will not necessarily be rewarded in this world."

One turning point that led Cash to put his Christian faith front and center was his friendship with Billy Graham, often considered the most influential preacher of the twentieth century. "No American revivalist before or since achieved the success that Billy Graham did in the middle years of the twentieth century," wrote Pulitzer Prize-winning historian Frances FitzGerald. In the late '60s and early '70s, when Graham was at the peak of his fame and power, and Cash had recommitted to religion after shaking his addiction, the two men connected: Cash invited Graham to appear on his television show (much to the dismay of his network superiors), and Graham invited Cash to be a part of his Crusade events.

"I wanted to understand that friendship," says John Carter Cash, "so I went to Billy and I said, 'What was it?' And he said, 'We were just brothers in Christ.' " But when Rick Rubin wanted to run the photo of Cash giving the finger to the camera at San Quentin as an ad in Billboard magazine to gloat about the GRAMMY won by the *Unchained* album, Cash said he needed to check with Graham. ""Billy said, 'I don't see anything wrong with it,' so it was OK—but that didn't have anything to do with 'brothers in Christ.'"

As the two men grew older, their friendship continued and strengthened. Together with their wives, they visited one another's homes and spent vacations together at Cash's property in Jamaica. Cash said that Graham encouraged him to "put my heart and soul into all my music," and described one

Cash's personal scrapbook photos from his visit to Israel, 1974. John Carter Cash, age four, is in the first photo.

Cash made this cross out of olive wood and shells that he collected at the Sea of Galilee while shooting *The Gospel Road* in 1971. He displayed it, along with a container of sand and more shells gathered at the same time, in his office.

conversation in which the reverend "challenged me to challenge others, to try to use what talent we have to write something inspiring." The next night, he said, he sat down and wrote "What Is Truth," a 1970 hit that spoke up in support of young people and their challenge to the establishment—"The ones that you're calling wild/Are going to be the leaders in a little while," Cash sang. "This old world's wakin' to a new born day."

Inspired by Graham, Cash and June enrolled in Bible study correspondence courses. "I learned just enough to understand that I knew almost nothing," he wrote, but his religious education remained a lifelong obsession; he collected Bible concordances and frequently used these indices to cross-reference and chase down different interpretations and analyses of the text.

The largest-scale project Cash took on—religiously oriented or otherwise—was the film and soundtrack *The Gospel Road*, which he

conceived of, organized, and paid for himself. The film was a narration of the life of Jesus, set in the biblical landscapes Johnny and June had previously described on their *Holy Land* album. The movie opens with Cash on a mountaintop (Mount Arbel, near the Sea of Galilee) holding a Bible and inviting viewers to join him in a journey through the Holy Land in the footsteps of Jesus.

"As Cash intones the words, 'This is My beloved Son, in Whom I am well pleased,' it's easy to imagine that God must have a Southern accent," wrote Richard Corliss in *Time* magazine in 2009, when the publication listed *The Gospel Road* as one of the Top 10 Jesus Films of all time. "The pauper-budgeted simplicity and good intentions of *Gospel Road* overwhelm the weirdness of a movie in which the director (blue-eyed, blond-haired Robert Elfstrom) plays Jesus and the star's wife is Mary Magdalene."

In 2014, in the Jewish online magazine *Tablet*, Shalom Goldman wrote an analysis of

The Gospel Road that considered the specific interest Cash and other "Christian pilgrims" to Israel held in the country. "American evangelical enthusiasm for Israel was about Jesus and the history of Christianity, not about the modern Jewish experience—though the Jewish 'return to the land' is understood by many Christians as the fulfillment of prophecy."

The film was released in March of 1973 (the same year as Godspell, a much higher-profile movie musical about Jesus), and though it was a commercial flop, it had a long afterlife on college campuses in the South and the Midwest, with screenings sponsored by the Campus Crusade for Christ.

"In the movie's climactic Passion section," Corliss wrote, "Jesus is lashed, kicked and spat on a few clumsy times, then totes his cross up a deserted city street. He dies in close-up, and the camera pulls back to reveal a modern American city (L.A.? Nashville?)—a strange but potent payoff, indicating that the Savior

died not only for the sins committed up to His time but for the ones we are still committing."

The critic found the right lesson in Cash's broad-stroke goals. As Cash's own fame and platform grew, he was increasingly interested in reaching young people with his message. He acknowledged the bad reputation that Christianity had with more progressive youth in the modern world, and understood how it had happened. "They've got to have some kind of foundations and moral principles to their lives," he said. "And I think they can find it in the Bible . . . but they don't have to relate to the bad things that have been done in the name of Christianity."

June, meanwhile, described the burden that her husband was feeling. "His shoulders get heavy because he feels a responsibility for young people," she said.

One rather silly effort made toward youth was Hello, I'm Johnny Cash, a comic book issued in 1976 by the Christian-themed pub-

Crown of thorns worn by Robert Elfstrom, who played the role of Jesus in The Gospel Road. Some of his blood is still visible on the prop.

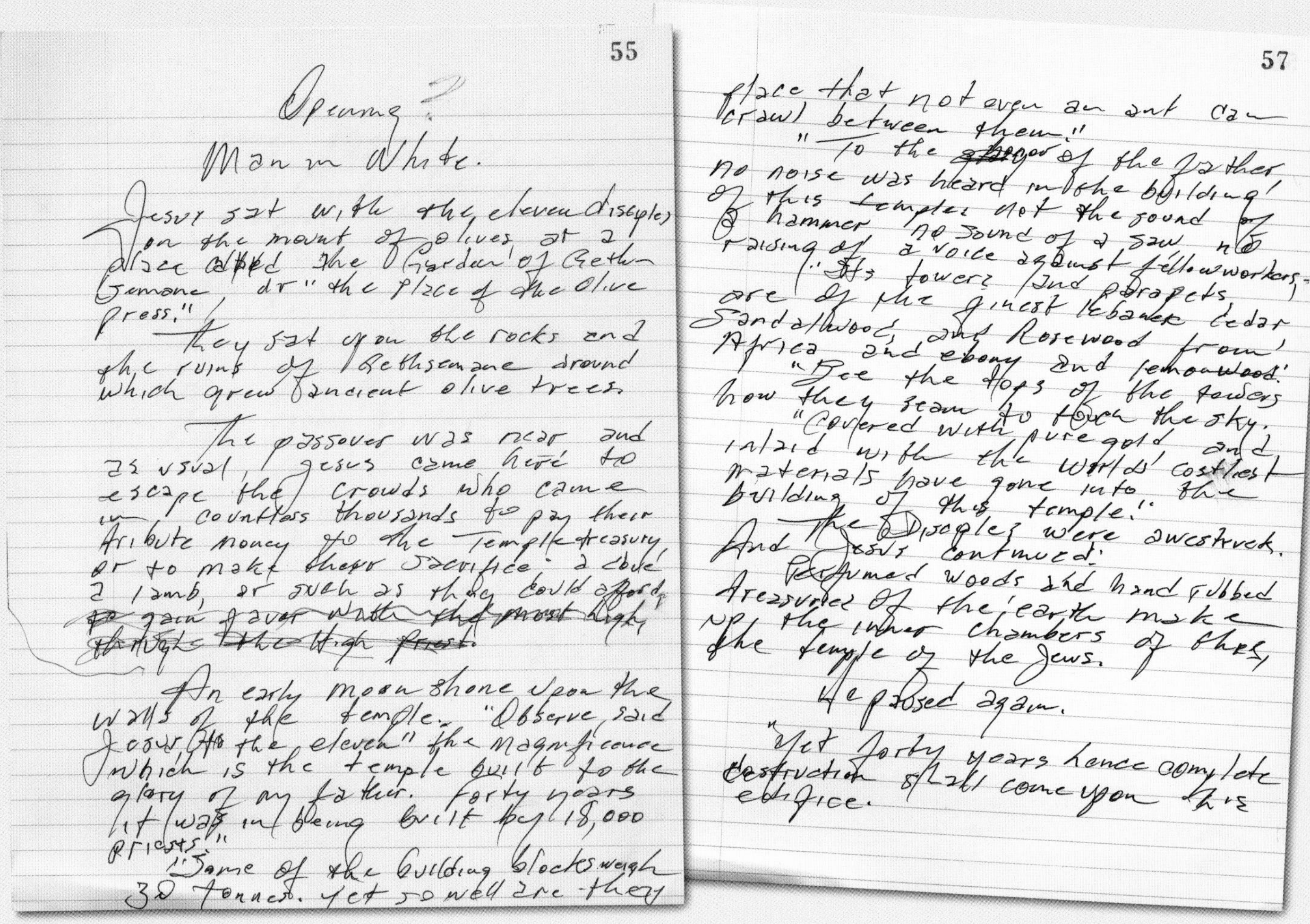

[Handwritten manuscript page 55:]

Opening?

Man in White.

Jesus sat with the eleven disciples on the mount of olives, at a place called the "Garden of Gethsemane," or "the place of the olive press."

They sat upon the rocks and the ruins of Bethsemane around which grew ancient olive trees.

The passover was near and as usual, Jesus came here to escape the crowds who came in countless thousands to pay their tribute money to the Temple treasury or to make their sacrifice, a dove a lamb, or such as they could afford to gain favor with the most high through the high priest.

An early moon shone upon the walls of the temple. "Observe," said Jesus to the eleven, "the magnificence which is the temple built to the glory of my father. Forty years it was in being built by 18,000 priests."

"Some of the building blocks weigh 30 tonnes, yet so well are they

[Handwritten manuscript page 57:]

placed that not even an ant can crawl between them."

"To the glory of the father no noise was heard in the building of this temple, not the sound of hammer, no sound of a saw, no raising of a voice against fellow-workers."

"Its towers and parapets are of the finest Lebanese cedar, Sandalwood, and Rosewood from Africa and ebony and lemonwoods."

"See the tops of the towers, how they seem to touch the sky."

"Covered with pure gold, and inlaid with the worlds costliest materials have gone into the building of this temple."

The disciples were awestruck.

And Jesus continued:

Perfumed woods and hand rubbed treasures of the earth make up the inner chambers of this, the temple of the Jews.

He paused again.

"Yet forty years hence complete destruction shall come upon this edifice.

Cash spent nine years studying and writing about St. Paul for the only novel he wrote, 1986's *Man in White.*

lisher Spire Comics. (Many of their comic books involved Archie and his friends at Riverdale High.) The comic related the ups and downs of Cash's life story in a campy, overblown style, climaxing in his marriage to June Carter and his religious salvation. The final panels featured a quote from Proverbs—"Train up a child in the way he should go: and when he is old, he will not depart from it"—followed by the cartoon image of Cash saying "This scripture is true in my life! I tried a lot of roads—but I came back to the one way I knew as a child—and Jesus, my Lord and Savior, made me whole!!!"

Ten years later, Cash published his work of fiction, *Man in White.* He claimed that he had spent nine years studying and writing about the life of St. Paul and his journey from Saul of Tarsus, enemy of Christ, to true believer. The historical novel gained a following among Christian bookstores and reading groups, though critics singled out the introduction (which *Kirkus Reviews* called "rambling . . . [but] at least alive") for praise. In this

first-person section, Cash recounts a dream he had the day before his father's funeral. He saw his Daddy get out of a long silver car, dressed in a blue suit, white shirt, and burgundy tie, happy in the hereafter. When he told his mother, she smiled "a smile of joy that comes from knowing a loved one is at peace and with God."

John Carter Cash points out that this book-length commitment to Bible study wasn't an anomaly for his father, whose curiosity about and focus on the text only increased with the years. "He was a scholar," he says. "He could tell you what page a description of Christ was on—the Bible wasn't just a book that sat on a shelf and looked pretty. I have thirty-, forty-page handwritten treatments on the book of Job that he did. He loved to learn, and he loved to share."

Cash continued to release gospel albums for independent religious labels as he bounced from Columbia to Mercury to not having a record deal. In 2000, he released *Return to the Promised Land*, the soundtrack to a 45-minute video filmed in Israel in 1990 as a "twenty years later"

This is my personal bible.
If found, please return to:

Johnny Cash
's House of CASH
Box 508
Hendersonville, Tn. 37075

follow-up to *The Gospel Road* that never made it to television.Only 2,000 copies of the CD were released, as advance orders and for media review; the Renaissance label shut down just two months after the album's projected release, and no additional copies were ever manufactured.

Return to the Promised Land was the last religious-themed album Cash would release in his lifetime. But spiritual themes and biblical language remained central to the work of his final years. "The Man Comes Around," the title track to the fourth album in the "American Recordings" series, was one of the last songs he wrote—a dense, elaborate meditation packed with obscure references from the Bible.

The song began as a dream that he was in Buckingham Palace, and the queen said, "Johnny Cash, you're just like a thorn tree in a whirlwind." Fascinated by the odd phrase, he dug into his concordances and found a mention of a whirlwind in the book of Job. When he actually started writing the song, he told me, "I came to the ultimate test of man and his obsti-

nacy, which is Judgment Day." As he worked on the song over several years, lines and phrases from the book of Revelation appeared, and the line "kick against the pricks" relates to Paul's conversion, as told in Acts.

"I closed the Bible one day and said 'the man comes around,' just said it out loud one morning," he told me. "I wrote dozens and dozens of verses—I thought it was just going to be one of my weird poems, but I started seeing a song forming."

Exploring, learning, evolving—this is what religion meant to Johnny Cash. He chose love and compassion over self-righteousness. And rather than finding conflict between his fights for justice and his undying faith, or pit his different constituencies against each other, he was able to build bridges, maintain his allegiance to society's underdogs, and serve as an imperfect, inspiring role model.

"To go into church is great," he once said, "but to go out and put it all into action, that's where it's all at."

Cash's analysis of the Bible informed his own writing throughout his career. To him, "the Bible wasn't just a book that sat on a shelf and looked pretty," his son, John Carter Cash, has said.

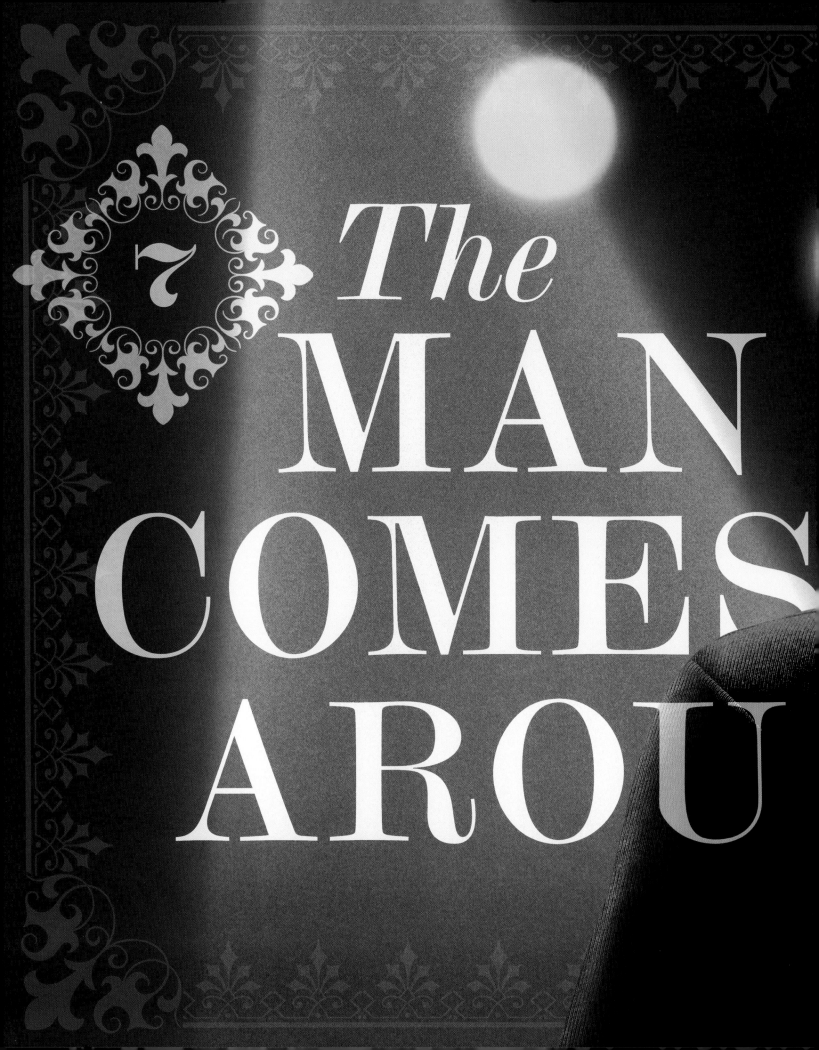

7 *The* MAN COMES AROU

ND

1993–2003

"**I** was spinning my wheels," Cash told me. "I'd been dropped by Sony, dropped by Mercury. And then one night, Rick came to my dressing room."

Rick Rubin had cofounded Def Jam Records out of his New York University dorm room. He produced LL Cool J and the Beastie Boys for his label, but the Long Island-bred metalhead and punk fan was drawn to more than just hip-hop. In 1988, he spun off of his own label, Def American, to which he signed such acts as the Black Crowes and Sir Mix-a-Lot, while also taking on production work for the Red Hot Chili Peppers and the Cult. By 1993, he had tired of the rap superlative "def," and changed his company name to American Recordings.

"At my current label, I had only ever worked with new bands," Rubin told *Vanity Fair*'s David Kamp. "But as a producer, I had gotten to work with grown-up artists. And I just thought it'd be nice to find the right grown-up artist who, maybe, is in the wrong place, who I could really do something great with. And the first person who came to mind was John. He already had legendary status, and maybe had been in a place where he hadn't been doing his best work for a while."

Rubin contacted Cash's manager, Lou Robin, to set up a meeting. Robin had no idea who the surprisingly quiet, Los Angeles-based rocker with the massive beard was, but he arranged a visit when Cash's tour brought him to Santa Ana, in Orange County. Backstage after the show, the two men shook hands, sat down, and then stared at each other for two silent minutes.

Cash with Rick Rubin and Tom Petty during the *Unchained* recording
sessions at Sound City Studios, Van Nuys, Californina, 1996

Eventually, Cash asked Rubin, "What are you going to do with me that
nobody else has been able to do to sell records with me?" Rubin's response,
Cash told NPR, was, "Well, I don't know that we *will* sell records. I would like
you to go with me and sit in my living room with a guitar and two micro-
phones and just sing to your heart's content, everything you ever wanted
to record."

"I told Rick about the *Johnny Cash: Late and Alone* concept I had," he
told me. "We had an audition in his house, in his living room, with his dogs
running around at my feet—and then we made our first record that way."

For weeks, the two of them sat together in Rubin's home, and Cash played
through dozens of songs—new, old, sacred, secular, originals, covers—while
the producer recorded it all and tried to assess what they might actually do
together. Eventually, Rubin began suggesting material as well, steered by
the image of the Man in Black.

At breakfast in Hendersonville with (left to right) U2 bassist Adam Clayton, Doug Caldwell, Jack Clement, and Bono, 1992; the next year, Cash would record "The Wanderer" with U2.

"The Man in Black was a big part of who he was in real life, as well as a mythical image associated with him," he said. "I would always try to find songs that were suited for that." Cash was willing to roll with Rubin's direction—"I had nothing to lose and everything to gain," he said.

The initial thought was to flesh out the songs with a basic band sound, and Rubin started bringing in various musician friends and associates to work up arrangements. But after trying different combinations, he realized that the acoustic demos were the right way to present these songs and this artist, at this moment. He suggested that Cash perform a set by himself, maybe a surprise show at a club, to see how it felt to play this material on a stage. Cash agreed but was nervous about the idea—after all, he had never performed solo before.

Rubin called his friend Johnny Depp, and they booked a show a few nights later in the Viper Room, the actor's tiny Sunset Strip club. In front of an invited audience that included Tom Petty, members of the Chili Peppers, and Sean Penn, Depp stepped onstage and said, "You know, I never thought I'd get to say this, but here's Johnny Cash!" The crowd's reaction made it clear that this lean, stripped-down approach, and the darker sensibility of the songs they had settled on, was resonating. The versions of "Tennessee Stud" and Loudon Wainwright III's "The Man Who Couldn't Cry" recorded at the Viper Room were actually selected for the album—which was titled, simply enough, *American Recordings*, when it was released in April 1994.

The album drew from a wide range of sources—from songs Cash had recorded in the '60s to tracks written specifically for the project by Tom Waits and Glenn Danzig. The album's scope, wrote Cash, "was all the music that made me.... [I'd] come full-circle, back to the bare bones of my music, pre-stardom, pre-electric, pre-Memphis."

"Everything was there," says John Carter Cash of the *American Recordings* album, "from the humor to the darkness, to the love for my mother, to the unsettled emptiness, to the hope and the gospel—and that's as much a part of what made that album what it was as anything."

It opened with the bleak humor of the murder ballad "Delia's Gone," for which Cash gamely filmed a stylized music video featuring Kate Moss. For this recording of "Delia," Cash noted in his autobiography, "I sent myself to the same mental place where I found 'Folsom Prison Blues' and being older and wiser to human depravity, picked up on some darker secrets than I'd seen in 1956." Brutal themes of death and violence coursed through the album; Cash noted that many of the songs were "bleak, and stark, and some of 'em kind of bloody. But that's American folk music."

American Recordings didn't explode on the charts (peaking at Number 23 on the country side, Number 110 in the Top 200), but the reviews were mostly ecstatic. In a five-star review in *Rolling Stone*, Anthony DeCurtis called the album "at once monumental and viscerally intimate, fiercely true to the legend of Johnny Cash and entirely contemporary." The *Chicago Tribune*'s Greg Kot praised the "quagmire of humor and bloodshed, pathos and treachery evoked by these songs."

Not all critics were completely sold on *American Recordings*, however; some felt that it reduced Cash to a one-dimensional badass and flattened the range of his work to a proto-gangsta cartoon. The *Chicago Reader*'s Chris Dickinson called the album a "masterful marketing tool" that "staggers under its own self-consciousness." In his book *In the Country of Country*, Nicholas Dawidoff described a "vague strain of self-parody coursing through *American Recordings*." But these were dissenting opinions; showcases at the South by Southwest conference in Austin and at the downtown Manhattan club Fez, and an appearance at the Glastonbury Festival, all added to the sense that there was a new Johnny Cash emerging. The album placed in the Top 10 on numerous critics' polls and went on to win a GRAMMY for Best Contemporary Folk Album.

Custom model Martin 000,
with a tree of life inlay on its
fretboard and headstock, made
for Cash in 1983

A 1972 Martin D-35, custom-made for Cash and autographed by Gene Autry, is said to be the first black-finished Martin guitar ever made. Cash used it on the road and for recording.

When I spoke to Cash, almost ten years into the remarkable renaissance that Rubin had triggered, he compared the producer to the visionary who had jump-started his career back in Memphis. "What I felt like was happening back then at Sun is a lot like what it felt like when I was starting with American Recordings," he said. "That something was happening out there, and I wasn't sure about what it was, but it felt good whatever it is.

"The thing that binds Rick Rubin and Sam Phillips together is that both men have vision," he continued. "They tell you how things are going to be because they see those things, they can see the future and the possibilities and that you haven't attained those things that they can see.

"When I first started recording with Rick, word got out that I was 'happening,' whatever that meant," he told me. "But I felt it was—like something really *was* happening. It felt really good to know that there was a possibility that I had an audience among the young people out there who were buying records."

With everything that was going on, the third and final Highwaymen album, *The Road Goes on Forever*, while perfectly solid, felt like a bit of an anticlimax, if not a step backward. By the fall of 1995, Cash was back in the studio with Rubin, this time chasing a slightly different sound. Tom Petty had called Rubin and asked if he could play bass on Cash's next recording sessions. When the producer asked Cash, he replied, "Tell him to bring 'em all!"

And with that, Tom Petty and the Heartbreakers—one of America's greatest rock and roll groups—became the house band for the second Cash-Rubin collaboration. Marty Stuart—not just a guitarist, but also a country music historian of the rock and roll generation (and Cash's former son-in-law)—acted as a link, a translator between the two musical traditions.

Petty would look back on these recordings as a career highlight. "I still view that as the best work we ever did," he said. "[Cash] had such an interest in so many kinds of songs.... He pulled the best music out of us that anyone ever has."

Other guests also participated in the album that would be titled *Unchained* (the only of the "American Recordings" series that didn't use the "American" label in its name). Flea from the Red Hot Chili Peppers and Fleetwood Mac's Lindsey Buckingham and Mick Fleetwood also turn up in the credits.

The material was even more daring than the selections on *American Recordings*. There were songs by Beck and the alternative rock band Spain. Most surprising, though, was the inclusion of "Rusty Cage" by Seattle hard rockers Soundgarden. "When I played Johnny the Soundgarden version, he was horrified," Rubin told David Kamp. "He thought I was insane. He just looked at me like 'What are you thinking? Have you really gone off the deep end? I don't think I can sing that.'" But Rubin heard something in Chris Cornell's raging expression of tension and escape ("When the forest burns along the road/Like God's eyes in my headlights"), so he cut a demo version

Album Feb. 22nd '94
Melbourne Aust.

Side One

1	1. Delias Gone	*
3	2. The Beast in Me	*
2	3. Let the Train Blow the Whistle	* Cabin?
4	4. Drive On	*
7	5. East Virginia Blues	*
6	6. Why Me Lord	*
5	7. Thirteen	*
	8. Bury me Not	*

Side 2

9	Bird On a Wire	* Fast? Best Cut?
10	Redemption	* Best Cut? Cabin?
11	Like a Soldier	*
12	Tennessee Stud.	* Guitar!
13	If I Give my Soul	*
14	Go On Blues	* cabin?
15	Down There by the Train	*
16	Old Chunk Of Coal	*

ABOVE Notes Cash wrote while finalizing the track listing and final versions of songs for *American Recordings*, 1994. OPPOSITE Rubin would send Cash CDs of songs that he wanted him to consider for the "American Recordings" series; the producer pitched Nine Inch Nails' "Hurt," one of Cash's defining moments, three separate times.

american™

american recordings inc. 8920 sunset boulevard, 2nd floor, los angeles, ca 90069 u.s.a.   telephone: 310.288.5300 fax: 310.288.5306

1/3/02

John,

Here is a cd of the five songs that we will concentrate on in the next round of recordings:

1. First Time Ever – Roberta Flack
2. Imagine – John Lennon
3. Bridge Over Troubled Water – Simon & Garfunkel
4. Hurt – Nine Inch Nails
5. Personal Jesus – Depeche Mode

Please listen to these songs every day, so when it comes time to cut them, you'll be confident.

Another three songs that we can catch are ones that you already know; Streets of Laredo, Father & Son – Cat Stevens, and No Expectations – The Stones. (We'll send lyric sheets for them anyway.)

Happy New Year! And I hope you are enjoying the Jamaican winter. Look forward to seeing you soon!

Peace,
Rick

of what he envisioned, with him singing and Chili Peppers' guitarist Dave Navarro playing behind him, and Cash was won over.

Cash continued to struggle with his health. The pain in his jaw from the unsuccessful oral surgery had increased, and he was pushing it down with painkillers. He admitted that he was developing "too much of a taste for Percodan, two or three an hour." Rubin said that the *Unchained* sessions marked "the first time we had seen him not feeling well, where he had to lie down on a couch for a while before he could sing again."

Even coming off of the hype and the accolades for *American Recordings*, the full-band sound of *Unchained* didn't see much more commercial success. After it won the 1997 GRAMMY for Best Country Album, Cash and Rubin took out a full-page ad in *Billboard* that reprinted the photograph of Cash flipping the bird to the camera at San Quentin, with this accompanying text: "American Recordings and Johnny Cash would like to acknowledge the Nashville music establishment and country radio for your support."

THE CREATIVE REBIRTH OF JOHNNY CASH CONTINUED, but following the release of *Unchained*, his physical problems worsened dramatically. His appearance was changing alarmingly quickly—his hair falling out, his forehead veins bulging, his body stooped, his hands trembling.

Around 1996, he began presenting symptoms that suggested Parkinson's disease—shakes, disorientation, dizziness, a general weakness. He rallied sufficiently to record the charming *VH1 Storytellers* television performance and live album with Willie Nelson, which saw the two legends, alone onstage with their guitars, trading songs and stories and sounding both remarkably casual and surprisingly powerful. He also voiced a memorable cameo for *The Simpsons*, in the character of a "space coyote" who served as Homer's spiritual guide during a psychedelic trip from extra-hot peppers at a chili-eating contest.

Later in 1997, he caught double pneumonia, and his lungs were so weak that he had to be put on a ventilator. He was put in a medically induced coma, to give his lungs a chance to heal, but when the doctors tried to bring him out, they were unable to rouse him.

The family gathered around his hospital bed, fearing the worst, and organized prayer vigils—"and within a matter of hours," June later recalled, "he just started squeezin' my hand." Eventually, Cash was diagnosed with diabetic autonomic neuropathy, which is not a specific disease but a collection of symptoms caused by nerve damage and affecting his blood pressure, respiration, and vision.

Cash was forced to give up touring, and whereas the first two albums with Rubin were recorded in Los Angeles, he would thenceforth work primarily in the Cash Cabin studio in Hendersonville. He put a good face on the need to curtail his travels. "I was on the road for forty years," he told me in 2001, "and now that I don't tour I can push my creativity in making records, which is my first love."

He did turn up onstage one memorable night in New York City. On April 6, 1999, *An All-Star Tribute to Johnny Cash* was filmed at the Hammerstein Ballroom for a special on the TNT network. Artists including Sheryl Crow, Wyclef Jean, Willie Nelson, and Dave Matthews—all wearing black—performed Cash songs live, while Bob Dylan, U2, and Bruce Springsteen contributed videos of their own Cash covers. June sang a spare, haunting version of "Ring of Fire," playing her signature instrument, an autoharp.

Until the last minute, no one knew whether the man being honored would take the stage. When the lights went up to reveal Cash at center stage, backed by a quartet including Marshall Grant and W. S. Holland, the room exploded. His performances of "Folsom Prison Blues" and "I Walk the Line" would be his final appearance on a big stage.

In 2000, Cash went back into the studio for the first time in four years to begin work on his third album with Rubin. It was hard not to hear many of the songs selected as anything but a response to his illness—most obviously, Tom Petty's "I Won't Back Down" but also Cash's own "I'm Leavin' Now" or the almost-century-old minstrel song "Nobody."

The changes to his voice were noticeable, the effort required to get the work done was palpable. It lent the album an undeniable emotional force, though the album—released as *American III: Solitary Man*—is the least essential of the "American" series. In *Rolling Stone*, Ben Ratliff wrote that "even the best good ideas can get pushed too far," describing the recordings as "offhand drawing-room performances."

Once again, the album was a GRAMMY winner, this time for Best Male Country Vocal Performance for Cash's version of the title track, written by Neil Diamond. It was also his highest-charting album since 1976, reaching Number 11 on the country rankings, but Cash expressed concern over the lack of bigger commercial success.

"I'm getting good write-ups and I'm proud of the albums," he said, "but they're not really selling all that much compared to the other acts that Rick works with. So I felt I was overstaying my welcome with Rick."

When I spoke to Cash a few months after the release of *Solitary Man*, his voice was shaky but his spirit was strong. "The illness sharpened my focus," he said. "Being idle, my brain wouldn't slow down. I was always thinking about those songs." He explained his choice to record Nick Cave's apocalyptic execution tale "The Mercy Seat"—"I did a show at the Tennessee State Prison one time, and I walked by the electric chair and a chill came over me. I thought about that feeling when I first heard that song"—and he offered his support for the "alternative country" scene that had sprouted in the '90s. "Alternative country had to happen, because the record business is in danger of overplasticization," he said. "You don't have to live in Nashville to record a country song—in fact, I'm not even sure it helps."

Between scheduled recording sessions, Cash was constantly listening for potential new material. "I listen to everything that people bring me—

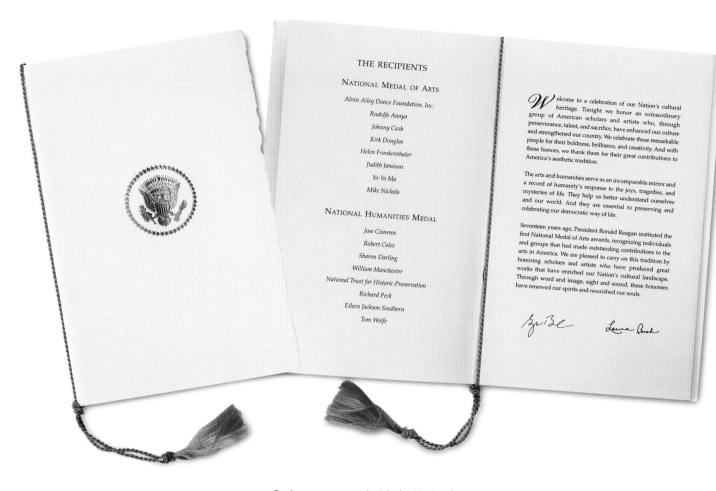

THE RECIPIENTS

NATIONAL MEDAL OF ARTS

Alvin Ailey Dance Foundation, Inc.

Rudolfo Anaya

Johnny Cash

Kirk Douglas

Helen Frankenthaler

Judith Jamison

Yo-Yo Ma

Mike Nichols

NATIONAL HUMANITIES MEDAL

Jose Cisneros

Robert Coles

Sharon Darling

William Manchester

National Trust for Historic Preservation

Richard Peck

Eileen Jackson Southern

Tom Wolfe

Welcome to a celebration of our Nation's cultural heritage. Tonight we honor an extraordinary group of American scholars and artists who, through perseverance, talent, and sacrifice, have enhanced our culture and strengthened our country. We celebrate these remarkable people for their boldness, brilliance, and creativity. And with these honors, we thank them for their great contributions to America's aesthetic tradition.

The arts and humanities serve as an incomparable mirror and a record of humanity's response to the joys, tragedies, and mysteries of life. They help us better understand ourselves and our world. And they are essential to preserving and celebrating our democratic way of life.

Seventeen years ago, President Ronald Reagan instituted the first National Medal of Arts awards, recognizing individuals and groups that had made outstanding contributions to the arts in America. We are pleased to carry on this tradition by honoring scholars and artists who have produced great works that have enriched our Nation's cultural landscape. Through word and image, sight and sound, these honorees have renewed our spirits and nourished our souls.

ABOVE Cash was presented with the National Medal of Arts in 2001 for "his remarkable musical innovations that drew from folk, country, and rock and roll styles." **OPPOSITE** Cash with President George W. Bush and First Lady Laura Bush

Rick, John Carter, the engineers, I listen to them all and try to respond to everybody," he told me. "I get my coffee early in the morning and usually every morning I listen to some music, usually to songs that were submitted to me the day before. It's a painful process of weeding them out."

By the time he started work on the fourth installment of the "American" series, "his body was weaker, but his psyche was stronger," according to Rick Rubin. If the tone of *American III: Solitary Man* was one of defiance, the songs on *American IV: The Man Comes Around* added in a bit more anger, and perhaps more desolation. Some choices felt almost too obvious—"Bridge Over Troubled Water," "In My Life," "I'm So Lonesome I Could Cry"—until you heard the depths Cash found in them. Other selections—Depeche Mode's "Personal Jesus" or Sting's "I Hung My Head"—were among the most daring of the Rubin recordings.

Cash explained his method of selecting material to record. "The way I approach a song, I have to love the song up front first," he said, "but I knew

that with some of these songs, I couldn't sing them the way they were recorded—and I didn't want to sing them that way, I wanted to sing them my way. I wanted to make them my songs. If it doesn't begin to feel that way, I just throw it out.

"Every album has had kind of a theme," Cash told me. "This time, the theme is spirit—the human spirit more than the spiritual or godly spirit, the human spirit fighting for survival. It probably reflects a little of the maturity that I've experienced, with the pain that I've suffered with the illnesses that brought me so close to death."

He was proud of the chances he took on the album and the effort he put in. "We put more blood, sweat, and tears and love into this one than anything we've ever done," he said. They recorded "Danny Boy" at a church in Los Angeles, with a massive pipe organ and natural echo. The Hank Williams song was cut with Nick Cave and just a couple of guitars. For the title track, he said, "I've never had a writing project that I put in as much time on as I did on that song. I wrote dozens and dozens of verses—I knew I was overwriting, but I had to do it, had to get it out."

Cash said that "Personal Jesus" fit squarely into his body of work. "That's probably the most evangelical gospel song I ever recorded. I don't know that the writer meant it to be that, but I could relate to it from the very beginning."

The Cash Cabin in Hendersonville, Tennessee. This photo shows a view from the original room, built by Johnny, into the new studio, built by John Carter. The last portrait ever taken of Cash, by Marty Stuart, hangs on the far wall.

And then there was the song that would, in some ways, redefine Johnny Cash's entire career. Trent Reznor's industrial-goth band Nine Inch Nails had recorded "Hurt" on their 1994 breakthrough *The Downward Spiral*, a concept album chronicling the descent of a man through depression to attempted suicide. Once again, Rubin heard something in the clear-eyed despair of the lyrics that led him to bring it to Cash.

"It's a strange song," said Rubin. "I mean, the opening line is 'I hurt myself today.' It's such a strange thing to say. And then the next line is 'To see if I still feel....' So it's self-inflicted. It's such a strange thought to open a song with." Reznor was skeptical of having Cash record "Hurt," thinking it would just be "gimmicky," while John Carter Cash, who knew the original, was mystified.

Rubin pitched the song to Cash on three of the CDs of potential material that he compiled for Cash to consider; after not getting any response the first two times, he wrote a note: "I think this particular song is a really special one. I feel like the words have a lot of power, and with you singing them it's going to take on a whole new light." When Cash still said he couldn't hear himself doing the song, Rubin assembled some musicians and, as he had done with "Rusty Cage," recorded a demo to illustrate his vision of an arrangement.

Cash told me that he once he could hear past the sonic assault of Nine Inch Nails, he keyed into the song's sense of a junkie examining his own destruction. "I think 'Hurt' is the best antidrug song I ever heard," he said. "If it doesn't scare you away from taking drugs, nothing will. And it's a song about a man's pain and what we're capable of doing to ourselves, and the possibility that we don't have to do that anymore. I never did the needle, never did that part, but I did everything else.

"It's talking about the pain and the hurt and the human spirit that overcomes—and all of us have gone through the hard times and know what we speak of when we speak of these things."

David Kamp described Cash's delivery of the lines "What have I become/ My sweetest friend/Everyone I know goes away in the end" and its contrast to Reznor's cold detachment. "In Cash's version, with his pitch wobbling uncertainly over the words 'What have I become,' the singer became an old man lamenting his mortality and frailty, feeling he's outlived his usefulness."

Rubin's friend Mark Romanek, who had directed landmark music videos for Michael Jackson, Lenny Kravitz, and Madonna, had been begging the producer for the chance to do something with Cash. Rubin played him three songs from *The Man Comes Around*—the title track, "Danny Boy," and "Hurt"— and he immediately seized on the Nine Inch Nails cover. "The initial conception was to do a somewhat stylized piece—in Los Angeles, at a soundstage— and it was going to be based very loosely on imagery from Samuel Beckett plays," says Romanek. "We were going to have some cameos of people like Beck and Johnny Depp." But Cash wasn't feeling up to travel for work, and in a few days, he was scheduled to go to his home in Jamaica, where he always went when the Tennessee weather turned colder and tempted pneumonia.

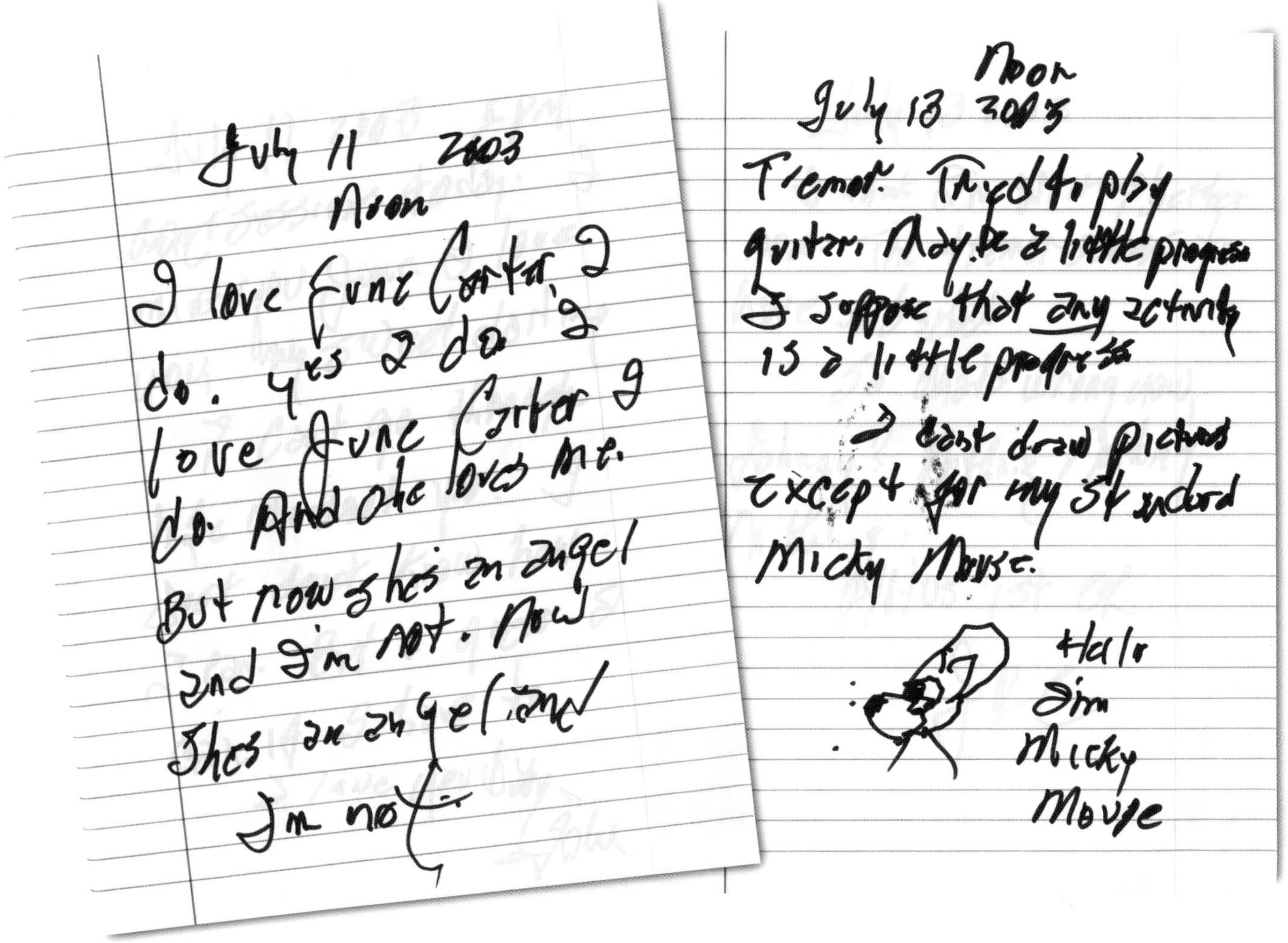

July 11 2003
Noon

I love June Carter I
do. Yes I do I
love June Carter I
do. And she loves me.

But now she's an angel
and I'm not. Now
She's an angel and
I'm not.

July 13 Noon 2003

Tremor. Tried to play
guitar. Maybe a little progress
I suppose that any activity
is a little progress

I can't draw pictures
except for my standard
Micky Mouse.

Halo
I'm
Micky
Mouse

Cash's journal from 2003, two months before his death,
reveals his struggle with June's passing ("Now she's an
angel") and the physical challenges of playing guitar.

Romanek would have to go to Cash and come up with an idea in or around Hendersonville. Rubin suggested that he look at the House of Cash, the roadside building in Hendersonville where Cash kept his offices and where his mother, who died in 1991, used to run a small museum of his memorabilia. "It had been closed since the Eighties; there was water damage everywhere," said Romanek; "When I saw the place was in such a state of dereliction, that's when I got the idea that maybe we could be extremely candid about the state of Johnny's health, as candid about the state of Johnny's life at this moment as Johnny has always been in his songs."

The sight of Cash intoning the agonizing, self-reflective lyrics of "Hurt" surrounded by the mess and chaos of stuff accumulated over a lifetime was shocking, unforgettable. For the final shot, Romanek told Cash to feel free to improvise, break something, whatever felt right; the singer said he had an idea, and slowly poured out a bottle of wine that was sitting on the table, conjuring an image of seeping blood.

At one point, June looked in on the proceedings from the staircase leading to the living room where they were shooting. "I glanced over and I saw June on the stairs," said Romanek, "looking down at her husband with this incredibly complex look on her face—filled with love and earnestness and pride, and a certain amount of sadness." With her permission, Romanek included a couple of shots of her, and the love and concern in her expression were painfully intimate.

Back in Los Angeles, Romanek's editors pulled up some photos and footage of Cash in his prime, and cut them into the scenes of the singer in the darkened, ruined living room. As powerful as the new shots were on their own, with this contrast "Hurt" became a meditation on mortality and legacy unlike anything ever attempted in the fast and loose world of music video.

The "Hurt" video "really upset me and it really affected me," said Rubin. "I thought it was beautiful, but it was so unlike any video I'd seen before, and so extreme that it really took my breath away, and not in a good way. I didn't know how to handle it; it was just overwhelming."

"I cried like a baby when I saw it, I was sobbing," said Rosanne Cash. "June was just sitting there, just watching it, patting me. See, they had a kind of an unflinching eye. They weren't sentimental in that way. It's like, they're artists—they use their life for their work." When daughter Kathy Cash broke into tears watching the clip, her father just said, "Aw, that's art! It's part of life."

"My dad was like a kid," said John Carter Cash. "He was like, 'This is great! Everybody's going to love this!' I'm not kidding. He was just so excited because he saw that it was a masterpiece."

With a personal push from Rubin, rock station KROQ in Los Angeles tried spinning "Hurt," and the listeners responded. Soon, other stations started adding the song, and it gained enough momentum that MTV took a chance on the video—so dramatically unlike anything they were showing. The next week, album sales doubled; by a few weeks later, they had doubled again, and soon *The Man Comes Around* would be certified Gold.

"Hurt" had become a phenomenon. *Time* magazine named it one of the 30 Best Music Videos of All Time; *Rolling Stone* readers chose it as one of the 10 Best Music Videos of the 2000s and one of the Top 10 Greatest Cover Songs of All Time (second only to Jimi Hendrix's version of Bob Dylan's "All Along the Watchtower"). In England, NME picked it as the greatest music video ever made. It was nominated for six MTV Video Music awards.

CASH WAS ENJOYING AN UNPRECEDENTED NEW CHAPTER in his career, a rebirth unlike anything pop music had ever seen. But for once, June, his greatest ally and partner, would not be savoring his success alongside him.

In early May of 2003, June was admitted to the hospital for surgery to replace a heart valve. She suffered a coronary arrest a few days later and passed away on May 15. After all of the attention given to Cash's health over the previous decade, it would be his wife who was gone first.

"I think my mother knew very well that she was a lot sicker than everybody else thought she was," said John Carter Cash. "I think she believed that she was not long for this world."

Rick Rubin spoke to Cash less than an hour after June passed away and said that he had never heard such pain and despair in Cash's voice. "At some point," said Rubin, "I asked him, 'Do you think you could look inside, somewhere, and find some faith?' And when I said that, it was like he became a different person. He went from this meek, shaky voice to a strong, powerful voice, and he said, 'My faith is unshakable!'"

After June died, Cash threw himself fully into his music, recording and writing as much as his body could handle. On the way back from the funeral, he turned to John Carter Cash and said, "I gotta get into the studio." Four days later, they were recording a song for a tribute album to the Carter Family that John Carter was assembling. Cash cut a little-known song called "I Found You Among the Roses"—the opening line is "Once again dear, it's rose time, it's June time." He had selected this song before his wife's death, but, says John Carter, in his state, "I don't think he realized what the lyrics meant."

Cash told Rubin, "I want to work every day, and I need you to have something for me to do every day. Because if I don't have something to focus on, I'm gonna die." And work he did. "There's still a pretty good hunk of music [from then] that hasn't been heard," says John Carter Cash. "We did a session with bluegrass musicians at the cabin that hasn't been heard. In the face of adversity and in the face of darkness and his body giving up on him, he not only endured, but he flourished."

On July 5, 2003, Cash went to perform at the Carter Family Fold in Hiltons, Virginia, just a short distance from Bristol—a town known as the "Birthplace of Country Music" because acts including the Carter Family made some of the very first country recordings there. He was too weak to walk to the microphone on his own but insisted on not being brought up to the stage in a wheelchair, so two assistants helped him. He delivered a thirty-minute set, working through some of his greatest hits—"Folsom Prison Blues," "I Walk the Line," "Sunday Morning Coming Down"—before stopping to reflect on his late wife, one of the Carter Family's own.

"The spirit of June Carter overshadows me tonight," he said. "With the love she had for me and the love I have for her, we connect somewhere between here and Heaven. She came down for a short visit tonight, I guess, from Heaven, to visit with me tonight and give me courage and inspiration, like she always has."

He followed with June's signature composition, "Ring of Fire," and a lively version of "Big River," after which he pointed out that the Fold usually only allows acoustic instruments on its stage. He said that cousin Janette

Carter had told the audience, "I know we don't allow anybody to plug in when they're here, but June said that Johnny Cash was already plugged in when she met him."

Cash closed with a song he had not performed onstage for twenty-five years, 1964's "Understand Your Man." Initially written as a warning to Vivian Liberto, now the song read as a tribute to June. He would not play onstage again.

On August 21, he went into the Cash Cabin to record. In the morning, he cut "Like the 309," the last song he ever wrote. The full impact of his version of "I Found You Among the Roses" had eventually caught up with him, and he asked John Carter if he could use a different song for the Carter Family tribute. They came up with A. P. Carter's "Engine 143," about an engineer rushing to reach the station on time; instead, he crashes his train and dies. (The recording would be nominated for a GRAMMY for Best Male Country Vocal Performance, and *The Unbroken Circle: The Musical Heritage of the Carter Family* earned three nominations.) It also happened to be the first song that June Carter ever sang live on the radio, when she was nine years old.

""Like the 309" and "Engine 143"—like the first single he recorded, "Hey Porter"; or the song that sparked his greatest popularity, the live version of "Folsom Prison Blues"; or even that poem he wrote for A. J. Henson, way back in high school in Dyess—were about trains. "Engine 143" ends with the line "And the very last words poor Georgie said was 'nearer, my God, to Thee.'" This was the final thing Cash ever recorded.

Cash was determined to attend MTV's Video Music Awards program on August 28. He was mostly confined to a wheelchair and barely able to see because of diabetes-related glaucoma. Rubin, though, had come across the works of a doctor named Phil Maffetone who specialized in devising comprehensive nutrition and exercise programs for extreme athletes, and in a short time, Maffetone had Cash walking unaided again and improving in general.

Nevertheless, when the awards came around, Cash's regular doctors decided that he wasn't healthy enough to travel to New York. In the meantime, Rubin had found out that "Hurt" wasn't going to win any of the big categories in which it was nominated (it won only one trophy, for best cinematography). When Memphis-born Justin Timberlake's "Cry Me a River" won for Best Male Video, he said in his acceptance speech, "This is a travesty! I demand a recount. My grandfather raised me on Johnny Cash, I think he deserves this more than any of us here tonight." (Both "Hurt" and "Cry Me a River" lost in the Video of the Year category to Missy Elliott's "Work It.")

By early September, Cash was hospitalized again, this time for pancreatitis, yet another complication of the diabetes. Cash spoke to Rubin on the phone, promising that he would come out to Los Angeles soon to work on the next album. But he didn't pull through, and on September 12, 2003, at the age of seventy-one, Johnny Cash passed away.

A view of the Cash Cabin studio

"I just don't have any fear of death," he wrote in the autobiography. "I have no regrets, I carry no guilt, and I have no ill will toward anybody."

Before he was gone, the "American Recordings" series had introduced his work to a new generation, and breathed a new context and vitality into one of music's greatest bodies of work. Rick Rubin had brought the various strands of Cash's interests and influences together, and revealed new dimensions to his artistry. The series created a template for all recording artists as they aged and contemplated their own legacies.

"It's like Matisse doing the jazz dancers when he was in his eighties," said Rosanne Cash of her father's latter-day work. "Like a whole new level of art and depth and mastery and confidence."

To me, Cash expressed a modest assessment of his final work. "It's been a really joyful period of growth artistically for me," he said.

"His life was like a tug of war," said Rick Rubin. "But for the time I was with him, his last ten years or so, he was on the winning side of the rope."

I STILL
MISS
SOME

8

LEGACY

ONE

THIS PAGE The case of
Mother Maybelle Carter's
1933 Stromberg guitar,
which she played while on
the road with Johnny

PREVIOUS Cash poses for a
portrait, Los Angeles, 2002

LEGACY

When I sat with Johnny Cash in 2002 in the Cash Cabin, he had recently celebrated his seventieth birthday and was approaching his fiftieth anniversary as a recording artist. He said that he was grateful for the attention and good wishes that the occasions had inspired.

"On my seventieth birthday, I got calls from all over the world," he said. "I had a nice day with all my old friends and people I love. I thought, 'The whole world seems to be having a birthday party in my name tonight, and I'm going to bed early!'"

But, he said, reaching these landmarks was no reason to slow down. "We don't polish milestones," he said, "we look forward to the next one—the fifty-first year, the seventy-first year. We look forward to the work to be done in that year."

Around the same time, he told *Rolling Stone*'s Jason Fine that "I'd die if I retire. Like like a shark—got to keep moving."

And, in fact, Cash's output did not stop with his death, nor has the public's fascination with his life and all that it symbolized. Carefully curated albums and writings that were unreleased during his lifetime continue to emerge, as do tellings and retellings of his story across numerous media.

The first selection of recordings from Cash's burst of creativity following June's death was released on July 4, 2006, as *American V: A Hundred Highways*. He had chosen and finalized this lineup of songs prior to his death, and it is a difficult, powerful document of a man staring down his imminent

Kris Kristofferson and Norah Jones performing onstage during the *I Walk the Line: A Night for Johnny Cash* musical tribute at the Pantages Theatre, Los Angeles, October 25, 2005

demise, the relentless and inevitable conclusion to a historic career capped by a remarkable decade-long creative renaissance. It was also Cash's first album to hit Number One on the pop charts in thirty-seven years.

A Hundred Highways is an old man's album; it is hard to think of any recordings that have made less of an attempt to hide frailness and physical pain from the microphone. Often, the listener's response is to hope that the singer can simply make it through the song—in "Like the 309," he wheezes "asthma coming down like the 309."

There's nothing on the album as surprising as "Hurt" or "Personal Jesus" or "Rusty Cage." Instead there is cohesiveness, a single-minded sense of purpose. Some titles make their intentions obvious ("God's Gonna Cut You Down," "I'm Free From the Chain Gang Now"), whereas other songs assume added meaning; the folksy Ian and Sylvia tune, "Four Strong Winds," popularized by Neil Young's version, drills down to one line—"Our good times are all gone/And I'm bound for moving on."

In 2010, the release of *American VI: Ain't No Grave* marked the conclusion of the "American Recordings" series—for now; in 2014, John Carter Cash said that in addition to more releases along the lines of the *Unearthed* box set of "American" outtakes, "there may be three or four albums worth of 'American Recordings' stuff, but some of it may never see the light of day." The ten songs on *Ain't No Grave* focused on Nashville standards and traditional material and, again, the specter of death loomed over the proceedings. In the *Los Angeles Times*, Ann Powers called the album "Cash's hospice record."

The lone original composition is "I Corinthians 15:55," based on the biblical passage "O Death, where is they sting? O grave, where is thy victory?" In a moving, light touch, the album's final song is Hawaii's famous "Aloha Oe" (Farewell to thee), which has been performed over the years by everyone from Bing Crosby to Elvis Presley to Bugs Bunny.

But Cash's own recordings are hardly the only way he has remained present in our culture since his passing. Even before the first posthumous album came out, the *Walk the Line* film had introduced the story of Johnny and June to a massive new audience of moviegoers.

In an appearance on Conan O'Brien's talk show, Joaquin Phoenix, who played Johnny in the film, recounted the one startling exchange he had with Cash. "I was invited over to dinner at his friend's house, and went over and it was an amazing experience," he said. "John and June were just beautiful people, and they sang this song together and looked in each other's eyes, and it was this beautiful spiritual. And then I had to leave, and John stopped me as I was walking out, and he was a real fan of this movie I did called *Gladiator*. And he said ... 'My favorite part is when you said your [Maximus's] son squealed like a girl when they nailed him to the cross and your wife moaned like a whore as they ravaged her again and again and again—I love that part!'"

Opening in November 2005, *Walk the Line* received rave reviews and was nominated for five Oscars, with Reese Witherspoon taking home the trophy for Best Actress. Phoenix and Witherspoon also won Golden Globes for Best Actor and Best Actress in a Musical or Comedy. They both performed their own vocals in the film (their version of "Jackson" was released as a single), and Phoenix, who learned to play guitar for the role, picked up a GRAMMY for his contributions to the soundtrack. The film, which had a $28 million budget, grossed more than $120 million in the United States alone, making it the all-time highest grossing music biopic until the hip-hop group N.W.A.'s story *Straight Outta Compton* surpassed it in 2015.

The toughest audience for *Walk the Line* was Rosanne Cash, who was especially troubled by the scenes depicting her mother, Vivian Liberto. "The movie was painful," she said. "The three of them [in the film] were not recognizable to me as my parents in any way. But the scenes were recognizable, and the storyline, so the whole thing was fraught with sadness because they all had just died, and I had this resistance to seeing the screen version of my childhood."

American Recordings IV: The Man Comes Around
was the final album to be released in Cash's lifetime.

John Carter Cash countered that, in his role as executive producer, he tried hard to avoid showing Vivian in a negative light. Mostly, he said, his parents had hoped for a movie that focused on their relationship, not their lives before they met. "What they wanted was a movie about their love, about their life together with God," he said. "I still stand strong and true and firmly that this is the movie that my parents together would have made."

A few months after *Walk the Line* opened, the songs of Johnny Cash made it to Broadway with a jukebox musical called *Ring of Fire*. Producer

PRESENTED TO
JOHNNY CASH
To commemorate sales of over
2,000,000 copies of the

COLUMBIA
LONG-PLAYING RECORD ALBUM
"Johnny Cash At San Quentin"

Columbia

RIAA CERTIFIED
Double Platinum

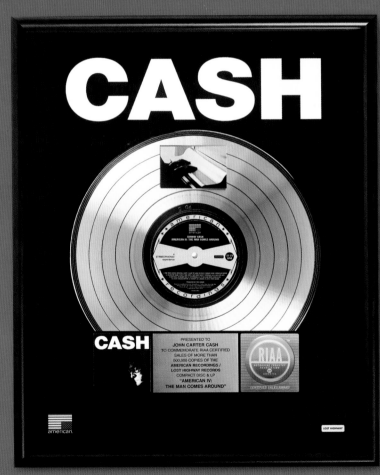

CASH

CASH

PRESENTED TO
JOHN CARTER CASH
TO COMMEMORATE RIAA CERTIFIED
SALES OF MORE THAN
500,000 COPIES OF THE
**AMERICAN RECORDINGS /
LOST HIGHWAY RECORDS**
COMPACT DISC & LP
"AMERICAN IV:
THE MAN COMES AROUND"

RIAA

CERTIFIED SALES AWARD

american

LOST HIGHWAY

NATIONAL ACADEMY OF RECORDING ARTS & SCIENCES

JOHNNY CASH

BEST COUNTRY VOCAL, MALE—1968
"FOLSOM PRISON BLUES"

OPPOSITE TOP Cash's Double Platinum award for 1969's *Johnny Cash at San Quentin* album, representing sales of two million copies, presented in 1986. The album has since achieved Triple Platinum status. **OPPOSITE BOTTOM** John Carter Cash's Gold record for his production on his father's epic *The Man Comes Around* album, which featured the memorable recording of "Hurt." **ABOVE** A selection of GRAMMY awards that Cash received, including 1968 Best Country Vocal Duo (with June) for "Jackson" and 2004 Best Music Video for "Hurt," filmed less than a year before his death.

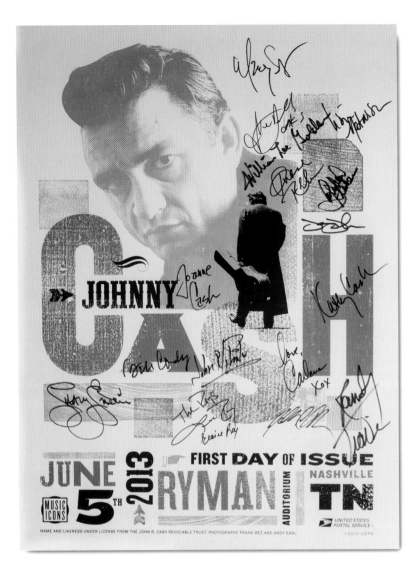

Limited-edition Hatch Show poster created to commemorate the US Postal Service's issuance of a Johnny Cash "Forever" stamp, signed by performers at the Ryman Auditorium concert and ceremony that celebrated the stamp's release date, Nashville, June 5, 2013. Hatch Show is a letterpress print shop in operation since 1879.

William Meade spent five years trying to persuade Cash to allow his music to be used for a stage production. Not long before he died, Cash agreed. "My father loved plays, and he'd seen many musicals," said John Carter Cash. "He felt honored, flattered that somebody with such talent and energy wanted to do this. He was excited both by the individuals involved and the idea of it."

Director Richard Maltby had previously conceived and directed the only two musical revues to win the Tony Award for Best Musical, 1978's *Ain't Misbehavin'* and 1999's *Fosse*. The Johnny Cash that he conveyed over the course of thirty-eight songs in *Ring of Fire* was a long way from the dark, gothic figure of the Rick Rubin albums; selections like "Look at Them Beans" and "Flushed From the Bathroom of Your Heart" revealed how unpredictable, goofy, and downright weird Cash could sometimes be.

"His writing kept going back to those really simple country images," Maltby said. "There is in that an American myth, and he lived it. It's almost archetypal, like Johnny Appleseed or Paul Bunyan: a young man leaving home, going out in the world, getting lost, going astray, finding his way back through Jesus and the love of a good woman. It's not everybody's Johnny Cash; it might not be anybody's Johnny Cash, but it's an essence that emerges from looking at what he wrote."

Unfortunately, the show clearly wasn't everybody's Johnny Cash; and indeed, it may not have been anybody's. Reviews were mixed, ticket sales were slow, and *Ring of Fire* closed after fifty-seven performances and thirty-eight previews.

But Cash would return to Broadway soon enough. *Million Dollar Quartet*, a musical built around the historic 1956 session at Sun Studio involving Cash, Elvis Presley, Jerry Lee Lewis, and Carl Perkins, premiered in 2010. The musical was nominated for three Tony awards, with Levi Kreis winning Best Featured Actor in a Musical for his portrayal of (the show-stealing) Jerry Lee Lewis. Cowritten by music historian Colin Escott, the show was modest in ambition but proved successful, especially as an ongoing touring property throughout the United States and Canada.

Other tributes to Cash came from less predictable directions. In 2013, the US Postal Service issued a stamp featuring a (circa 1963) photo of Cash. A rather freaky honor came in 2016, when a new species of black tarantula was identified near Folsom Prison and given the name *Aphonopelma johnnycashi.*

Years after his passing, Cash's music continues to be reissued, repackaged, and reexamined. New compilations, box sets, and live albums appear frequently, constantly adding to our knowledge of his profound body of work. After Cash's death in 2003, a massive stash of his handwritten notes and papers was discovered at the home in Hendersonville, with writings dating back to 1944. ("He never really threw anything away," said John Carter Cash. "Most of this was stored away in desk drawers in his office and filing cabinets in a storage room.") The younger Cash enlisted Pulitzer Prize–winning poet and Princeton professor Paul Muldoon to help go through this archive and select the most interesting pieces.

In 2016, forty-one of the approximately two hundred poems and song lyrics were published as *Forever Words: The Unknown Poems.* Some of the writings are almost painfully intimate. "You Never Knew My Mind," from 1967, expresses Cash's bitterness during his divorce from Vivian Liberto, and "Going, Going, Gone," from 1990, speaks directly and candidly about his drug abuse: "Liquid, tablet, capsule, powder/Fumes and smoke and vapor/ The payoff is the same in the end."

John Carter Cash points out one particular poem, which is reproduced on the back cover of *Forever Words*—an eight-line piece called "Forever," which Cash wrote just two months before he died, soon after June had passed:

You tell me that I must perish
Like the flowers that I cherish
Nothing remaining of my name
Nothing remembered of my fame
But the trees that I planted
Still are young
The songs I sang
Will still be sung

These words are recited by Kris Kristofferson to open the *Forever Words* album, released in 2018, which features an all-star cast of musicians who set sixteen of the previously unpublished lyrics to music. The lineup illustrates the range of influence that Cash had across musical genres—among the contributors are Chris Cornell (in one of his final recordings, paying back the favor of Cash recording "Rusty Cage"), Brad Paisley, Jewel, John Mellencamp, Elvis Costello, and even Rosanne Cash, who posted on Facebook that "I do very, very few projects related to my Dad, Johnny Cash, but I was so taken with the idea of this one, that I couldn't resist."

Whether musician or listener, we're still trying to fully make sense of Johnny Cash, still considering the kaleidoscopic elements that made up this remarkable man and his extraordinary work. Fifteen years gone, he continues to challenge and reward us.

"The iconic Johnny Cash image, at first, may baffle some," says John Carter Cash. "There are so many layers, and there are also misdirections and falsities. Can this mystery be revealed, the question 'Who was Johnny Cash?' I don't think it ever can be—because one of the essential mysteries is that he was a mystery unto himself."

Rosanne Cash insists that you cannot separate the man from his music. "In the smallest, most trivial events of daily life, he thought as a great artist . . . [with] trust, respect, and a wide-open mind," she said. "He was willing to live with the weight of his own pain without making anyone else pay for it." Elsewhere, his eldest daughter spoke of his "essential nature" as an artist—"the risk-taking and the rawness and the willingness to put all of the emotion, dark or light, on the line, nothing held back."

When I spoke to Johnny Cash in his cabin in the Tennessee woods, he was still thinking of his relationship to his fans. Though his days were numbered and he would only make it to a stage a few more times, he continued to stress his dedication to the people who had been listening to him for almost fifty years. "I make that commitment to every crowd, to every audience. I don't leave my audience no matter what the problems are."

"I won't leave you," he said, "if you won't leave me."

Recording booth in Cash Cabin, Hendersonville, Tennessee

ACKNOWLEDGMENTS

THANK YOU TO EVERYONE at the Smithsonian who first approached me about participating in this project and then made it a pleasure to navigate—Carolyn Gleason, Christina Wiginton, Jody Billert, Jaime Schwender, Leah Enser, Carla Borden, and Matt Litts. Rosanne Cash and John Carter Cash graciously shared their time and insight. I am honored that Josh Matas, Sandbox Entertainment, and the Johnny Cash Estate trusted me with such an important story. Dr. Ruth Hawkins and the Arkansas State University Heritage Sites program do a remarkable job with the Johnny Cash Heritage Festival in Dyess—go if you can. As always, Sarah Lazin is invaluable as an agent and as a friend. Thanks also to Margaret Shultz in Sarah's office. From a distant continent, the magnificent Alice Bezanson did extraordinary fact-checking work and offered laser-sharp editorial advice. Back in the day, Luke Lewis, Lauren Murphy Lewis, and Jim Flammia allowed me to spend that unforgettable day interviewing Johnny at the Cash Cabin. Thanks to Darlene Bieber and Brad Paisley, and to Kathy Kane and Pam Wertheimer, Roger Coletti, Mark Goodman, Nicole Krieger, Kerry Alivizatos, and the whole Volume channel at SiriusXM allow me to keep this kind of work going while somehow also doing daily radio. Eternal gratitude to Hal Brooks, Mike Errico, Dan Carey, Dick Schumacher, Jennifer Adams, Rob Johnson, Sam Kramer, and all the other friends who put up with me after all these years. Irwin, Janet, and Sharon Light have always given unconditional love and support. Thank you John R. Cash for the example of your music and your life. Suzanne and Adam, I love you so very much. Because you're mine, I walk the line.

THE JOHN R. CASH REVOCABLE TRUST would like to thank everyone at Smithsonian Enterprises, including Mark Bauman and Matt Litts. We thank Chloe Post and Ashley Gunnells at Sandbox Entertainment for their archival work, and the team at Loeb & Loeb—including Tiffany Dunn, Mary Lauren Teague, Melissa Hazel, and Amber Gilliland—for their guidance. Additional thanks to Trey Call, Kenan McGuffey, and Lauren Moore. Finally a massive thank-you to John Carter, Rosanne, Tommy, Joanne, and Damon for their time and effort to assemble this project and to all the Cash family members that have contributed their stories.

Photo shoot in driveway in front of
Cash home, Los Angeles, 1959

INDEX

Note: page numbers in **bold** indicate photographs.

PHOTO CREDITS

Unless noted below, all images are copyright the John R. Cash Revocable Trust

2–3: Getty Images / Michael Putland; **4–5**: Sony Music Archives / © J.T. Phillips; **6–7**: Sony Music Archives / Don Hunstein © Sony Music Entertainment; **11**: Getty Images / Bettmann; **15**: John R. Cash Revocable Trust, photographed by Nick McGinn; **16**: Getty Images / Beth Gwinn; **20**: Getty Images / ABC Photo Archives; **23**: Michael Hibblen / KUAR News; **24**: Sony Music Archives / Don Hunstein © Sony Music Entertainment; **27**: Library of Congress / © Joel Baldwin; **50**: Getty Images / Charles Peterson; **52L**: Getty Images / GAB Archive; **52R**: Getty Images / Bernard Hoffman; **53**: Getty Images / Michael Ochs Archives; **57**: Sony Music Archives / Don Hunstein © Sony Music Entertainment; **61**: Getty Images / Michael Ochs Archives; **62**: Getty Images / Colin Escott; **73**: Getty Images / Michael Ochs Archives; **74T**: Sun Entertainment Corporation; **79, 80–81**: Sony Music Archives / Don Hunstein © Sony Music Entertainment; **83**: Sony Music Archives / Hal Adams Photography, courtesy Suki Adams Sporer; **84**: Sony Music Archives / Don Hunstein © Sony Music Entertainment; **85L, 85R**: John R. Cash Revocable Trust, photographed by Nick McGinn; **87**: Getty Images / Country Music Hall of Fame and Museum; **91**: Getty Images / David Gahr; **94, 95**: John R. Cash Revocable Trust, photographed by Nick McGinn; **99**: Associated Press; **104**: Getty Images / Hulton Archive; **106**: Getty Images / Bettmann; **107**: Dan Poush; **110–111**: Getty Images / Bettmann; **113**: Sony Music Archives / Don Hunstein © Sony Music Entertainment; **117**: Dan Poush; **120–121**: John R. Cash Revocable Trust, photographed by Nick McGinn; **122**: Sony Music Archives / © Jim Marshall Photography LLC; **123**: Getty Images / Pictorial Parade; **124**: Sony Music Archives / © J.T. Phillips; **131**: Dan Poush; **132–133**: John R. Cash Revocable Trust, photographed by Nick McGinn; **137**: Getty Images / Jack Vartoogian; **141**: Getty Images / Bettmann; **149**: Getty Images / Pictorial Parade; **157**: Smithsonian National Portrait Gallery / © Jim Marshall Photography LLC; **160**: Associated Press / Mark Lennihan; **162B**: Getty Images / Paul Slade / Paris Match; **165**: John R. Cash Revocable Trust, photographed by Nick McGinn; **166L**: Getty Images / Peter Macdiarmid; **166R, 167, 169L, 169R**: John R. Cash Revocable Trust, photographed by Nick McGinn; **171**: Getty Images / Paul Natkin; **172–173**: © Alan Messer; **175**: © Kevin Estrada; **177, 178, 186L, 186R**: John R. Cash Revocable Trust, photographed by Nick McGinn; **187**: Getty Images / Stephen Jaffe / AFP; **188–189**: John R. Cash Revocable Trust, photographed by Nick McGinn; **195**: John R. Cash Revocable Trust, photographed by Nick McGinn; **197**: Getty Images / Harry Langdon **197**; **198–199**: John R. Cash Revocable Trust, photographed by Nick McGinn; **201**: Getty Images / Kevin Winter; **203**: Martyn Atkins; **204T, 204B, 205BL, 205TL, 205TM, 205TR, 205BR, 209**: John R. Cash Revocable Trust, photographed by Nick McGinn

For educational, business, or sales promotional use, please write: Special Markets,
Smithsonian Books, P. O. Box 37012, MRC 513, Washington, DC 20013

Published by Smithsonian Books
Director: Carolyn Gleason
Creative Director: Jody Billert
Senior Editor: Christina Wiginton
Editorial Assistant: Jaime Schwender

Edited by Carla M. Borden
Designed by Anderson Newton Design
Research assistance by Michael Pahn
Johnny Cash Historian: Mark Stielper
Manager, John R. Cash Revocable Trust: Josh Matas

Library of Congress Cataloging-in-Publication Data

Names: Light, Alan author.
Title: Johnny Cash : the life and legacy of the Man in Black / Alan Light.
Description: Washington, DC : Smithsonian Books, 2018. | Includes index.
Identifiers: LCCN 2018011525 | ISBN 9781588346391 (hardcover)
Subjects: LCSH: Cash, Johnny. | Country musicians--United States--Biography.
Classification: LCC ML420.C265 L54 2018 | DDC 782.421642092 [B] --dc23 LC record
available at https://lccn.loc.gov/2018011525

Manufactured in China, not at government expense

22 21 20 19 18   5 4 3 2 1

Images of Johnny Cash are used with permission of the John R. Cash Revocable Trust,
unless otherwise noted on page 215. Smithsonian Books does not retain reproduction
rights for these images individually, or maintain a file of addresses for sources.